WORK, PLAY, PRAY HARD

LIFE AND LEADERSHIP LESSONS
Of Visionary CEO Clark Baker

Carolyn S. Baker, EdD

Printed in the United States of America

Published 2019 by Carolyn S. Baker

Nashville, Tennessee

2nd Edition, 2019

ISBN 978-0-578-46072-7

Original cover design by David Read, Nashville, Tennessee

Professional photo contributions:
Jean-Paul Lavoie, Elon University, North Carolina
Kirsten Maloney, Falls Church, Virginia
Artist rendering of cover photo of Clark Baker--Shawn Carson, Houston School of Art
Larry Haney Whipple Portraits, Houston, Texas (author photograph)

Editor- Kendal Gladdish

Designer- Layne Moore

Time Line- Nick Simpson

WORK, PLAY, PRAY HARD can be purchased for business or promotional purposes.

For more information, please contact:
Carolyn S. Baker
207 Belclaire Place
Nashville, TN 37205
832-594-4078
Or email carolynbaker@sbcglobal.net

Proceeds from the sale of this book will be donated two YMCA camps: Camp Widjiwagan in Nashville, Tennessee, and Camp Cullen in Houston, Texas.

Printed and bound in The United States of America by Jostens Inc.

IN HONOR OF
VISIONARY LEADER

CLARK DAVID BAKER

Who happens to be my best friend

DEDICATED TO

BILL PHILLIPS
&
BILL WILSON

For supporting Clark's career

Clark's Career Timeline

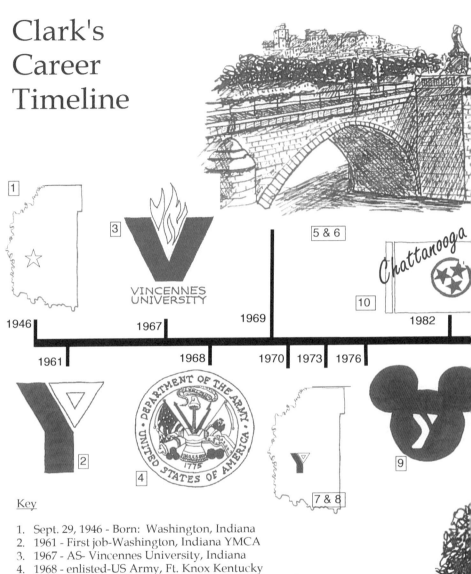

Key

1. Sept. 29, 1946 - Born: Washington, Indiana
2. 1961 - First job-Washington, Indiana YMCA
3. 1967 - AS- Vincennes University, Indiana
4. 1968 - enlisted-US Army, Ft. Knox Kentucky
5. 1969 - Assigned to US Army Europe, Heidelberg, Germany
6. 1969 - Met his wife, Carolyn, Heidelberg, Germany
7. 1970 - Named program director - Washington, Indiana YMCA
8. 1973 - Named Executive Director - Washington, Indiana YMCA.
9. 1976 - Chief Operation Officer (COO)- Central Florida YMCA, Orlando
10. 1982 - Chief Executive Officer (CEO) - YMCA Chattanooga, Tennessee
11. 1986 - BS degree-Covenant College, Lookout Mountain, TN
12. 1987 - CEO-Middle Tennessee YMCA, Nashville
13. 2001 - CEO-Greater Houston YMCA, Texas- 3rd largest Y in the nation
14. 2015 - Retires and moves to Nashville

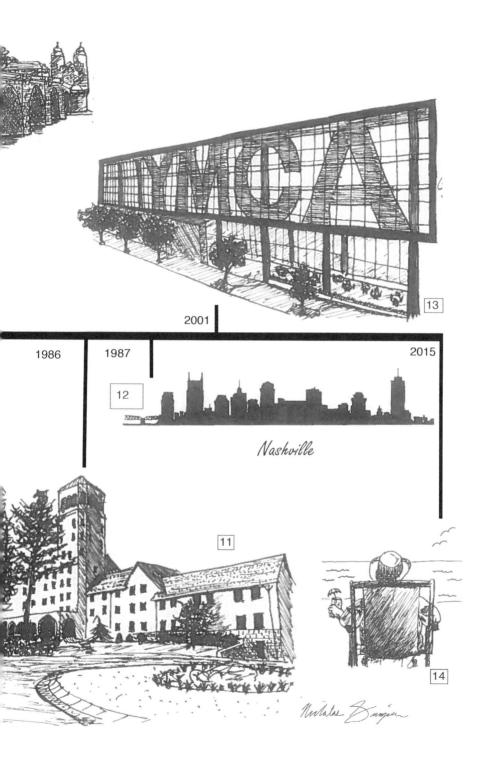

13

2001

1986   1987   2015

12

Nashville

11

14

TABLE OF CONTENTS

FOREWORD

Mark Twain said his idea of Hell was writing a Foreword for a book. "No one ever reads the Foreword," he said. I can't entirely blame anyone. You want to plunge right into reading the book.

If you're still with me, the book you are holding is the story of one of the most amazing men I have ever met. The reason the book is so fascinating is that the author is someone who knows him best of all— his soul mate, Carolyn.

If you haven't met Clark David Baker, you will meet an extraordinary human being in this book. If you do know him, you will find him on every page. He comes alive.

"Have a Clark Bar." That was my introduction to Clark about 20 years ago. The Clark Bar, by the way, is a heavenly confection of milk chocolate and peanut butter. Clark has given away thousands of these bars to new friends.

From those early days grew a friendship of over two decades. Each year, my esteem for him has grown— each year more than the year before. You will understand why when you read the book.

He is a fundraiser without parallel. He built nine new branch YMCAs and one camp in Nashville when he was CEO, and raised over $200 million for capital in Houston where he led the Y. It is his spirit and heart that makes him so effective.

The book could easily have been entitled something about leadership. Because that's what Clark is all about. A leader. An inspiring leader. He somehow gets people to climb fences they never thought possible. You'll read about this.

There is a chapter of Clark's life I did not know about. I bet even many of his close friends didn't either. Carolyn writes with total candor about the serious problem Clark had to face and how he dealt with it. Carolyn strips the bark from the tree.

Where Clark is at his very best is what we now call Human Relations. He loves people. That is a theme throughout the book. And I'm thinking, "And who doesn't like Clark? How can you not like him?"

In the book, I learned about the little boy from Washington, Indiana. He was given a scholarship at the YMCA. He has repaid that a thousand times over. Carolyn writes about all the lessons Clark has learned along the way.

You read about the little things that shaped his life. I love the part where he deals with a crisis. Clark says it is never a crisis. Only an opportunity. That is indeed his philosophy.

I'm reminded of a friend who worked at General Electric. He told me, "At GE, we are never allowed to talk about problems. We only have opportunities. But at times, we have a hell of a lot of opportunities."

You will read about Clark's passion for thanking people. There is a great lesson here. And another item is how he is compulsive about writing notes. He won't leave the office until he has written seven notes to friends. I've been on the receiving end of a lot of these. And I've saved them.

I love what Howard Schultz, CEO of Starbucks, said about his mission. "We're not in the coffee business serving people. We're in the people business serving coffee."

I can just hear Clark echoing the same. "The Y isn't in the gym and swim business serving people. We're in the people business of providing an amazing array of activities and programs that forever touch their lives."

His credo is: Play Hard, Pray Hard, Work Hard. He lives by that. Carolyn chose the perfect title for the book.

His love for the Church is a thread woven throughout the fabric of the book. And you learn about the extraordinary way he touches lives.

Now you are ready to dive into the book. You will have a joyful, inspiring journey. We can thank Carolyn for that.

Before you begin, just think for a moment of the thousands of lives Clark has touched. And the lives they have touched.

In this country, there are disciples of Clark's heading YMCAs in a dozen major cities. Former staff who went on to become CEOs. Clark was a model for them. A mentor. A coach. Consider the lives they touch.

I spoke to a person the other day who had once been on Clark's staff. He told me, "Clark was a powerful leader. Always thoughtful. A visionary. He motivated us to do things we never thought possible. The staff would walk through a wall for Clark."

When I think about Clark, I remember the story about Charles Laughton. Laughton was one of the great and best known actors of the 1950s and 1960s. It's said that Laughton was attending a Christmas party with a family in London. During the evening, the host asked everyone attending to recite a favorite passage that best represented the spirit of Christmas.

When it was Laughton's turn, he skillfully recited the 23rd Psalm. Everyone applauded his performance.

The last to participate was an adored, elderly aunt who had dozed off in a corner. Someone gently woke her, explained what was going on, and asked her to take part. She thought for a moment and began in her shaky voice, "The Lord is my shepherd, I shall not want . . . " When she finished everyone was in tears.

When it got time to leave, at the end of the evening, a member of the family thanked Laughton for coming and remarked about the difference in the response by the family to the two recitations of the Psalm. When they asked him his opinion, Laughton responded, "I know the Psalm. She knows the shepherd."

Clark Baker knows the shepherd.

Carolyn has given us a personal and confidential glimpse of this remarkable man. It is a book that had to be written. And no one could have portrayed him as effectively and intimately.

Clark's career might be summed up from Matthew 25:23:

"Well Done good and faithful servant."

JEROLD PANAS
Co-founder and Chairman – Institute for Charitable Giving
Executive partner – Jerold Panas, Linzy & Partners

PROLOGUE

My husband has an excellent reputation as a leader, especially in the nonprofit world. After 50 years of service he has been introduced numerous times as a "legend." He humbly responds, "That's because I'm old." But his leadership transcends old----what he's learned and the successes he has had are worthy of being put in print. I recall when the seeds of this book were planted.

We were on one of those lengthy drives to visit relatives back Indiana and Virginia. Clark began talking about wanting to put some tidbits of advice in writing where people could read through quickly and get ideas. While he drove I began to jot down these ideas. Shortly thereafter, my husband came up with a little pamphlet titled "Baker's Little Instruction Book." The subtitle was "A few bits of wisdom I have learned during my YMCA journey." There were 48 one-liners that my husband often quoted plus wisdom he felt others might be able to use. He would hand these out after some of his speeches. Many people would ask him for the little booklet, and the comments were very positive.

This got me to thinking about actually writing a book that would delve into these bits of wisdom, sharing stories which might help young people who might be interested in becoming successful leaders. I knew plenty of Clark's narratives from his countless speeches to various organizations. I attended quite a few and observed how audiences seemed to love these stories---they are like parables as they always had a good lesson. As I discussed the book idea with Clark, he seemed open to it. I told him it would have to be an "open book" as he would have to include the difficult times with the good.

"Look, you have overcome many obstacles and have succeeded", I said. "That is going to be very helpful and inspiring to many potential leaders to see that you are not perfect, but worked through your problems and came out a winner. In fact, those chapters sharing struggles might even be the most read as many people encounter problems in their lives. You can share through this book that success can happen inspite of obstacles."

Clark consented, allowing me to write even about the most personal, difficult times---times that he has shared with very few people. I'm proud of him for being open to the good and bad times in his career.

In September, 2013, I decided to send an email to all of Clark's contacts in his address book to ask for any memories of occasions when Clark taught them a lesson in leadership. His faithful executive assistant, Mary Norton, helped me. This book has been enriched by stories from an array of my husband's friends, board members, relatives, and former staff members from all over the nation. Their contributions have made the book more powerful and gives credence to his advice. I am grateful for every story, and each person who sent it.

I personally interviewed a number of people who worked closely with Clark. One of them was Chief Development Officer of the Nashville YMCA, Julie Sistrunk. Clark hired Julie to be his communications director while he was CEO in Nashville and now he works part time for her. Julie has spirit, energy, great ideas, and a strong work ethic. My husband could always count on her. Julie was the one who made me realize that when Clark talks about playing, praying, and working hard, he does so by doing all those things at the same time. She told me that he never differentiated between the three---while working hard, play was a part of it and so was prayer. That stood out to her. All this time, I was pondering how to separate the aspects of the title within the book. Julie helped me realize that all three occurred at the same time. I know that Bill

Wilson, Clark's former board chair, had told me that Clark made being part of a board fun. That is what helped to set him apart.

Coming up with a title was challenging. Our nephew and godchild, Jean-Paul Lavoie, was one of the first to respond about a title. He shared that "Play, Pray, Work Hard" is the mantra he remembers to this day.

I liked the title, but worried that it would not be strong enough. After three years of mulling around all sorts of ideas an event occurred that brought me back to my original thought. Clark had been asked to speak to a group at YMCA Blue Ridge Assembly. It is a gorgeous facility in the midst of the beautiful mountains of North Carolina. Kurt Stringfellow, CEO at the Y in Sarasota, had invited Clark to be the keynote speaker at his staff retreat. My husband asked me to join him. While Clark was speaking at the retreat he mentioned that his mantra has always been to work hard, play hard, pray hard. Suddenly Kurt whispered to someone, then tiptoed to the back of room where he opened a box and pulled out something green. At the time I thought it was impolite of him to distract people while Clark spoke.

He came over and sat down next to me to reveal a green

t-shirt he had printed that read: "PLAY, PRAY, WORK HARD." He said, "I'm giving these out to all my staff after this speech. I had no idea that your husband coined that phrase."

WOW---I felt as if this was my sign. It seemed that this phrase keeps coming back and I knew Clark would like it.

That's how the title came to be.

This book is written from my point of view. Any stories added from those participating in my request for stories are in off-set type or I have given credit to the writer. I worked hard to verify the facts, but like everything in life, people have different viewpoints. This book is mine.

The book contains 20 chapters, each having a subtitle which is advice that Clark believes is important to become a successful leader. Chapters begin with a key story but many include additional stories that support the highlighted advice. My epilogue speaks about retirement.

I thank Clark for allowing and encouraging me to write about his stellar career. After meeting this guy, my life has never been the same----after reading this book, I hope the same is true---that your career and your life will never be the same.

INTRODUCTION

A European Encounter – Clark Meets His Best Friend

Folk music was all the rage. It was 1967.

Specialist 4th Class Clark David Baker was stationed in Heidelberg, Germany. It was his first experience overseas and the first time being away from his beloved Hoosier roots. He found his Catholic faith was a way to meet new friends so he became very active in the Patton Chapel folk choir.

Living not far away in military housing was the Simpson family where my father had also been assigned to US Army European Headquarters. My sister, Dianna, and I attended weekly mass and loved all the new folk church music and were eager to get involved--- but where? Our local church did not seem interested in this "new" type of music, so we joined a group who were singing at another church, Patton Chapel. This is where both of our lives changed-Dianna met Allan (her husband of 45 years) and I met Clark (going on 44 years of marriage).

Clark played the organ and ukelele. In fact the entire group played "ukes".

I bought one and on our first date Clark began to teach me to play. We were babysitting for Dr. William Fleming and his wife, Elaine. They were the unofficial "parents" of the our new found friends. I'll never forget when I arrived home from my first date with Clark. Dianna couldn't wait to hear how it went---we shared the same bedroom and just about everything else. We were inseparable as sisters, so her opinion mattered to me.

"Well, how'd it go?" she inquired.

"It was great---I had a good time. He's just a great guy."

Good," she remarked, "I want him as a brother-in-law."

I was shocked that after one date, my sister seemed to see what was not even on my radar---marriage. Dianna was the first to like Clark, but my entire family grew to love him, except maybe the dog, who didn't want a stranger intruding on her territory. Clark charmed the entire Simpson family.

We began to date and I began to truly fall in love, not only with Heidelberg, but with Clark. On one of our many walks and drives to see the country, he shared his philosophy of life. It's a simple, yet poignant poem, *Live Each Day to the Fullest* by S.H. Payer

Live Each Day to the Fullest

*Get the most from each hour, each day, and each
age of your life.
Then you can look forward with confidence, and back
without regrets.
Be yourself, but be your best self.
Dare to be different and follow your own star.
Don't be afraid to be happy and enjoy what is beautiful.
Love with all your heart and soul. Believe that those
you love, love you.
When you are faced with a decision, make that decision as wisely as possible, then forget it.
The moment of absolute certainty never arrives.
Above all, remember that God helps those who help
themselves.
Act as if everything depended on you and pray as if
everything depended on God.*

I have treasured that poem since Clark shared it with me over 45 years ago. I have found that he truly lives by it and I believe is part of why he's been so successful. In fact, I borrowed his poem to take as my philosophy also.

How did this young man from Indiana come to meet his future bride in of all places---GERMANY?

Clark had lived in Washington, Indiana, all his life. His father, Carl, worked at a local factory. His mother, Rosemary, was a stay-at-home-mom. Clark was like an only child as his oldest brother, Dick, was 15 years older and his baby brother, Mike, was ten years younger. Clark attended the local community college, Vincennes University. He was living in his hometown and  happily working as program director at the local YMCA.

The Vietnam War was raging at the time, and Clark knew there was a good chance he'd be drafted. So, he decided to enlist to serve his time. After serving a year at Ft. Knox, he happened to receive two sets of orders in one day. One set assigned him to Germany; another to Vietnam. Which set of orders should he follow?

He phoned the commanding officer and presented him with the dilemma.

"Interesting. Look at the orders and tell me which has the earliest date," his officer directed.

"The orders to Germany, sir," the young soldier replied.

"Well, son, it looks like you're going to Germany."

So he packed his bags and headed overseas to Heidelberg where he worked for the United States Army European Headquarters in the AG (Office of the Adjutant General). He lived in Patton Barracks and attended church at the base Patton Chapel.

Meanwhile.....

I never wanted to go to Europe...I was IN college, IN love, and IN-volved with activities. My father was career military and received orders to go to Germany. For the first time in my life, I was at the age where I could have made the decision to stay in the United States where I strongly desired to finish my degree, but, having little money, I packed up with my parents and headed overseas with the rest of the family. My poor sister, Dianna, was headed for her senior year in a brand new school. Needless to say, she nor I were very pleased when we arrived in Germany. I can still recall the day—it was wet and dreary. I was thinking, "What did I get myself into?"

Our family had six children at the time so it was good that my mom had us to help with our younger siblings. Child number seven, Christopher, was born while we were in Germany. I smile when I recall my mother sharing the news that she was pregnant and naïve me saying, "But Mom, you can't be pregnant, you're 40!" Christopher and I are 20 years apart---he was the ring bearer in our wedding.

Heidelberg is truly one of the most beautiful, quaint cities in Europe, but living in drab fourth floor government housing---the charm didn't sink in right away.

Dianna and I decided to make the best of it. We worked as waitresses until we both acquired jobs as DACs (Department of Army Civilians). Basically, we were secretaries and enjoyed our jobs. I went to school at night so that I could finish college, knowing that it would be delayed because of the move.

It was during this time that my sister and I became involved with the Patton Chapel Choir. Our little Heidelberg choir became very close---we traveled together, celebrated together, and prayed together. Regardless of how late we had partied on Saturday night, come Sunday morning, we were all at Mass led by our director, JoEllen Armentor. Every other year we still gather from all over the country to have reunions.

I had taken night classes at the University of Maryland European Division and earned over 125 credits. I was determined to finish college and told Clark that was a priority even though he had recently proposed across from the romantic Heidelberg Castle. I returned to the states in 1970 to complete my degree at Longwood University in Farmville, Virginia. Clark returned to Indiana that same year to continue working for the Washington, Indiana YMCA as program director. Three years later he became the executive director.

After graduating with my bachelor's degree in education in May of 1972, Clark and I were married in June of that same year. I then moved to be with him in Indiana.

It was here that I began to realize that I had married a truly special man. He simply knew everyone in town. They all seemed to love this young man who was like a jack rabbit, hopping from place to place, being involved with the local folks.

My husband especially loved being near the Sisters of Providence who ran the very schools he had attended. Of course his favorite was his aunt, Sister Frances Joan. After I met her, we became fast friends and I will always see her as one of the most positive influences in my life. Love of God radiated from her. I never heard her say an unkind word. She was fun to be with and loved our children---she even became the godmother of our second child, Caroline.

The Washington Times-Herald

Clark Baker presented Jaycees' Distinguished Service Award

By GREG THOMAS

A lifetime Washington resident, Clark Baker, was honored Thursday by the Jaycees as the 1975 Distinguished Service Award winner. He was selected because of his work with local persons of all age groups.

Baker, Executive Director of the Davies County YMCA, is also a board member of the Community Concert Association, Area 13A Agency on Aging Advisory, Senior Citizens Housing Committee, Kiwanis, Washington Catholic Schools, and advisory board member of the Baster home for boys and president of the Washington Catholic Parent-Teacher Organization.

As a member of St. Simon's parish, Baker organized the Catholic Education Development Committee, be 1975-76 finance committee, the parish Choir, he co-organized and chaired the renovation committee of is a current member of the parish nance commission and of the liturgy planning committee.

Under his leadership the previous yr, the YMCA has opened the Whitney Aquatic Center, and marked record growth in membership and in expansion of programs in Daviess and Montgomery, and has opened the Retired Senior Volunteer program.

...resenting the award last night the dinner at the Moose Club, ...committee chairman Jerome ... said "Baker has affected, ... or influenced the life of ... in this room within the last ... and will continue to do so in ...ure. As sure as we here ... control the destiny of the ...er generation, so, too will the younger generation control ours. This native son has had a dynamic Christian influence on our youth."

Walker added that Baker is "a qualified, dedicated leader of this city and county. He is a man of vision for the future development of the community; a man with interest in all ages; a man who believes in the personal development and professional growth of his staff and himself, a man of tireless energy and a man of great integrity whose life exemplifies his Christian beliefs."

Other members of the selection committee were Mrs. John Williams and Jay Myers. Nominations were accepted from the general public and the decision was based on contributions to the general community welfare, evidence of leadership ability and of personal or business progress.

Paul R. Murphy, president of Evansville's National City Bank, in his address told the audience that community service is the rent "we pay for the space we occupy in society" and he went on to set out seven guidelines for achieving efficiency in community service.

Murphy challenged his listeners to accept a goal in life and believe in it and he said that if they do that their goals will become reality.

Jaycee president Mark Allison recapped the club's year, explaining some of the major projects which included the state Clyde award, initiation of Project Aware and sponsoring the March of Dimes Walkathon, Haunted House, Junior Achievement, the Cystic Fibrosis campaign and others.

JERRY WALKER, left, chairman of the selection committee, presents Clark Baker with the Jaycees annual Distinguished Service Award.

While in Indiana I also observed Clark's kindness to the elderly which was extraordinary for someone so young. Women's clubs and church groups loved to have him come and speak to their groups. He always obliged and did so loving every minute being with them. He could visit the nursing home where he knew many of the residents and bring cheer to all who were there. He got such joy from them---he would listen intently to their stories confirming the respect he had earned in Washington, Indiana. In 1976 he was the youngest person to receive the Jaycees' Distinguished Service Award.

I have always believed that Clark inherited his wit from his mother, Rosemary, who was quite the character, and his kindness from his father, Carl. His father had the sweetest disposition and when I would visit from college, he would always slip me a 20-dollar bill. It was so thoughtful and needed! His father passed away from cancer just weeks before our daughter, Christin, was born. It was so good to have new life around after such a loss.

His godmother, Marie Drew, was a true blessing to us during those early years. I had always stayed with Marie when I visited, and she bought me lovely outfits that helped clothe me during college. She and his Aunt Fannie and Uncle Albert Clark fixed us frequent dinners as we both worked. Even more important was they all were so present when our first child, Christin, was born. Uncle Albert used to take of care of little Christin and he just lit up when we drove up to drop her off---they would take walks, work in the garden, and swing. It was a special time. I guessed that's why I was shocked when Clark told me the summer of 1976 that he was ready to move.

What? Move from your beloved hometown? But he was ready for more adventures and felt that after completing a successful fundraising campaign and building a new indoor pool, it was time to move on.

Orlando, Florida, was our next move. CEO Bill Phillips hired my husband, and a newly formed close relationship began. Today, Clark and I are both so grateful that Bill insisted Clark begin to put money into the retirement fund. It was challenging to think about retirement when he was in his early 30's. Money was tight and we needed every penny just to live, but he listened and now we enjoy the blessings of Bill's wise counsel.

Clark was understanding about my wants and desires. In Florida I decided to work on a master's degree. My husband was very supportive and took on child care duties when I went to evening classes. It was a joyful day when I received my master's degree in education from Rollins College in 1978.

It was also in this city that our second child was born, Caroline. We now had four mouths to feed, but Florida began to blossom and the Y began to prosper so times were good. The Sunshine State had so many fantastic entertainment centers, not the least of which was Disney World. We had oodles of guests and made excursions to the Magic Kingdom on the average of once a month while we lived there. I could see that Clark's energy was in high gear. He became close to his staff at that time, especially Cindy Ferguson and Tina Harr. Both worked for the Y, but spent many great times at our home and helped to raise our girls. We left Florida in 1982 with "sand in our shoes"----so much so that we purchased a condo on the beach, sharing it with our longtime Heidelberg friends, Bill and Elaine Fleming. After 30 years, we continue to enjoy our place at New Smyrna Beach where we can now watch our grandchildren frolic on the same beach where we so fondly recall our own children doing the same.

Clark seems to have a keen sense of knowing when is the best time to leave. Not long after Bill Phillips moved to become CEO of the Seattle Y, our family found a new adventure in a state where I'd never lived----Tennessee.

I've cried every place I've left. Even though I was an Army brat, I got very attached to friends and to the schools where I taught. When Clark mentioned moving to Tennessee, I had reservations. But that's where we went. Clark was hired to be the CEO of the Chattanooga Y. And it worked out fine, just like it did when I moved to Germany and found my partner. Moving to Chattanooga was the beginning of a love affair with the state of Tennessee.

I believe I began to see Clark's gift to connect with board members in Chattanooga. He had to work with many people who had lived there all their lives and many were set in their ways. Yet, my husband managed to work with each person and get them involved, and he was able to inject new life into the Y.

One of the programs where he brought new life was in the area of aerobics. He added many classes and hired outstanding instructors and it became one of my favorite pastimes. They were so popular that an entire gym was necessary to house all the folks who worked out. Clark had the Y humming. After my classes I was totally refreshed before I picked up our girls who enjoyed the after school program in the same building.

Our six years in Chattanooga from 1982 to 1987 were special---we lived on Signal Mountain where the beauty of nature abounds. We lived right behind the school. I could grab my bags, walk through the woods, and in minutes I was at work. When our oldest daughter entered junior high, she began to take that same walk with me as she attended my school. My husband took our youngest daughter, Caroline, to the Catholic school on his way to work. It was most enriching until Clark sought to move up to a larger Y. He was invited to take the helm at the Nashville YMCA. He accepted, and we moved to the state's capital.

My energetic husband was excited about the opportunities---Nashville was growing and the Y was poised for expansion. It was here that I especially saw my husband's ability to surround himself with outstanding staff and forward-thinking board members. It was an exciting place to be. During his time in Music City, he built eight new YMCAs plus the Joe C. Davis Outdoor Center (home of Camp Widjiwagan) where you will find a building named after him: The Clark D. Baker Lodge.

During that time I wanted to expand my education. With Clark's support I enrolled at Peabody College of Vanderbilt University. The girls attended the Dominican campus schools and while working on my doctorate, I worked part-time (and later full time) for the sisters at Overbrook

School. After three years and a lot of hard work, I gratefully completed my Doctorate in Education (EdD) in 1993. This positioned me to be able to work on the college level. I taught a few classes at Aquinas College, but stayed at Overbrook as I loved my work there so much.

My life was enriched by two volunteer activities: 1) the founding of the Nashville Catholic Middle School Forensic League which recently celebrated its 25th anniversary, and 2) being a part of the founding of Pope John Paul II High School in Hendersonville. It was here I chaired the committee to hire the first headmaster.

In all of these activities, I gained wisdom from watching how Clark worked with boards and led a team. I listened and observed the way he accepted challenges with such grace. I was blessed that some of that poured into me; whenever a difficult situation occurred, I'd consult with Clark who always seemed to give me sage advice. I KNOW he helped me deal with many challenges, as well as teaching me how to celebrate the accomplishments of others.

We had been in Nashville for 14 years when Clark was encouraged to apply for CEO of the Greater Houston YMCA---the third largest Y in the nation. Nashville was now like home for us, but our girls were out of school and Clark felt he had one more move and instinctively knew he should go for the position. He accepted, and as empty nesters we moved to Houston.

I was overwhelmed with the size of this city. When someone tells you its bigger in Texas, they are not kidding! We called this move our great adventure. Bill Phillips, who was retiring as CEO there, had left the Y strong financially. Again the Y, like the city, was poised for growth. It was here where I saw Clark expand the Y, even in challenging times. He also was able to bring a satellite campus of Springfield College in Massachusetts to Houston. The campus has been successful in providing undergrad and graduate degree opportunities to the area.

Clark received Springfield's 2016 Humanics Achievement Award, which recognizes an individual "who has exhibited courage in the face of adversity, demonstrated leadership in service to others, advanced diversity and inclusion, served as a champion for the oppressed, furthered education in spirit, mind, and body, or contributed significantly to the understanding of the universe."

Preparing to receive the Humanics Achievement Award, Clark is photographed with David Snow (Development Director of the Houston Y) and his family at Springfield College, Massachusetts, May 2016.

Besides adding the Springfield College satellite campus, Clark led the city in building TEN new facilities and totally rebuilding Camp Cullen. Two of note are:

--The downtown Y, which required relocating residents and selling the old building. The new building has allowed the Y to expand its membership from 1,500 members to now nearly 10,000! At the time it was built this was the largest Y facility in the nation and is worth visiting.

--The Texans YMCA. It's the first YMCA in the nation sponsored by an NFL team. Built in the historic 3rd ward, it services one of Houston's most diverse communities.

I especially am proud of Clark as he accomplished much in spite of in-house challenges. His strong board and key supportive staff overcame obstacles and were success-ful--even during the economic recession that came razor close to plunging our country into a severe depression. In reflection, it is amazing the progress made in Houston. I learned from Clark that you don't dwell on the problems, but consider them opportunities.

Daughter, Christin, Carolyn and Clark at the Arts & Science Center dedication, June 2016

The last two projects that Clark wanted to complete before he left are near and dear to my heart. The first is the rebuilding of Camp Cullen after a disastrous fire in 2010 which completely destroyed its dining hall. Since the camp was in need of an overall restoration my spouse felt this was a good time to begin a campaign to build a brand new camp. After a successful campaign that began in 2010 after the fire and was completed in 2015, the rebuilt camp opened and became one of the finest in the area and draws more children each year. When Clark retired in 2016 they announced a building would be named The Carolyn and Clark Baker Science and Fine Arts Center. We were both humbled and surprised by the announcement.

The second project was the Miracle League complex---sports fields that are adapted for those with special needs. My brother, Mark, was born with Down syndrome, a developmental disability. Having a sibling with this condition has made me more sensitive to others with special needs. So I was thrilled when Clark embraced this campaign and we made a personal pledge to help.

The fields are made of materials that allow easy access for wheelchairs and soft falls. To attend a baseball game at the fields is so heartwarming. What I experienced at a game was the following:

Shawn Borzelleri, VP of programs in Houston, and Clark congratulate a Miracle League player.

* Dedicated Y staff and volunteers help and organize each game.
* Volunteers announce the child's name on a loud speaker system as each child steps up to the plate (just like in the major leagues).
* A song chosen by the child is played when each child comes to bat.
* Each child has volunteer "buddies" who help them on the field and while at bat. The buddies have told me they enjoy the game as much as the children with special needs.
* No team loses---the games always end in a tie.
* Even children with severe disabilities have smiles a mile wide.

I'm so proud of Clark who helped to coax our friends Harriet and Joe Foster to lead the campaign. Clark and I both know that without their support we would not have succeeded. I just know that had Mark been alive he would have thrived in this truly miracle league.

Carolyn with development officer, Linda Lycos, and philanthropists, Harriet and Joe Foster.

We left Houston feeling pleased that Clark was able to complete his time there with two meaningful and successful campaigns. Our great adventure had a happy ending. Clark and I made a mutual decision to return to Nashville for retirement. Our oldest daughter had recently moved back, and Caroline and her family were a short flight away. Plus my Virginia family would be an easy drive from the Tennessee city.

Clark quickly became involved with eight boards, serving as chair of the St. Thomas Hospital Health System. He also is continuing working in development---part-time with the Nashville Y.

I am involved again with the forensic league by judging for tournaments. I'm also on a committee to help bring a class for children with special needs to a Catholic school. Being asked to return as a board member for Pope John Paul II High School has been a nice reconnection. Of course, writing this book has been a goal and proceeds from the book will go to two camps that Clark and I both have fond memories of---The Joe C. Davis Center (which houses Camp Widjiwagan in Nashville) and Camp Cullen in Houston.

I learned much from my best friend---Clark lives, breathes, and yes, even sleeps YMCA. He is the embodiment of the Y mission. I went along for the ride and became a believer in his philosophy. He never had to lecture. I learned from watching his good actions.

I hope I continue to learn from this thoughtful leader, who I fell in love with over 45 years ago. He continues to WORK, PLAY, PRAY HARD.

Three past CEO's from Houston: Bev Laws, Clark Baker, Bill Phillips. Clark always remembered to invite former leaders, like Bev and Bill to YMCA events.

MRS. TROUSDALE'S LIFE-CHANGING GIFT
Honor the Past

It all started with Mrs. Beulah Trousdale.

Ten-year-old Clark Baker used to romp and play outside in Washington, Indiana. Never content to stay in his own yard he found himself wandering onto the neighbor's lawn. Mrs. Trousdale was passionate about her flower beds and she could see from her front window that this little boy was constantly in her yard stomping around in her beloved garden. She adored the child, but wanted somehow to find another place for him to play, thus saving her plants from being demolished.

One day Eugene Smith, the director of the local YMCA and a teacher, presented Clark with a little white piece of paper. It was a membership card to the YMCA where he could have fun meeting people and enjoy limitless activities. Mrs. Trousdale was the benefactor. The membership was $6 for one year (it was 1956 and that amount was no small gift). The little boy was ecstatic, and Mrs. Trousdale's flowers began to thrive once more.

Recently, Clark smiled at me and said, "I basically went to the Y one day and never came home.

That simple gift from Mrs. Trousdale began Clark's love and lifelong ties to the YMCA. I was fortunate to meet this diminutive, soft-spoken gentle woman before she left this world, and she spoke highly of her relationship with Clark. He is so appreciative of her friendship and the gift that changed his life. From those early years in his career to this day, Beulah Trousdale's framed photograph is prominently displayed in his office.

Clark never forgot the people, the pioneers, who built the foundation upon which he and other leaders now stand. Perhaps it was his love and connection with the elderly. For some unknown reason Clark has always loved older people---he enjoys talking with them, laughing with them, and listening to their stories.

My husband's favorite book, other than the Bible, is a rag tag antique. It's considered The Bible of the YMCA: the Young Men's Christian Association Handbook. I've seen him refer to and read from it many times. When he prepares a speech, out comes the YMCA Handbook. Much of what was written back inthe 1880s is still relevant, although some passages are quite humorous:

"Housekeeping…When stoves are used the janitor should be taught to keep everything tidy about them, using special care in handling the coal and ashes. If lamps are used they must be well trimmed, the fixtures clean, and the chimneys bright."

Others appropriate for any time frame:
"The success of a new association will depend largely upon the composition of its working committees, and especially upon the chairmen."

"Self-reliance. A man must believe in himself if he is to be a strong leader — must himself be confident if he is to inspire confidence in others."

"Enthusiasm. A genuine enthusiasm is both inspiration and strength. It is a cheer in the race, a song on the march, the battle cry in a charge. Enthusiasm is contagious---the leader will import it to others."

Perhaps because of this respect and understanding of the powerful heritage of the YMCA, plus growing up with fondness for older citizens, Clark always remembered to honor the past---those who brought us here. He always invited past CEOs to various events---annual meetings, dinners, and dedications. In fact, because of Clark, various buildings and special rooms are now named in honor of those CEOs who worked so diligently to keep the Y prominent in various communities. In 2014, the entire executive floor of the administrative center was named after Bev Laws, who was CEO in Houston, Texas, for 20 years. It was impressive to see how many people came to the dedication and how touched the former leader was, as he listened from his wheelchair. Less than a year later, Bev passed away. His wife Katie shared that one of the last things he was working on was writing a thank you to Clark. He didn't get a chance to finish it, but what Katie sent was very touching. My husband was so pleased to have honored Bev while he was still with us.

When I first met Clark, he spoke fondly of Albert Ice, his boss at the Y in Washington, Indiana. I couldn't wait to meet Albert who had such influence over this young man. Stepping off the airplane for my first visit to the Hoosier state in 1971, I couldn't wait to be introduced to this great star. After all the hyperbole of Clark's raves about Mr. Ice, I felt pretty sure he could walk on water. I was a bit taken back to shake hands with an older gentleman with white hair who shuffled around, constantly jingling change in his pocket. But, I quickly learned that my future husband had wisdom many years beyond his chronological age. Clark was a keen listener and follower of older folks----and Albert did indeed have much wisdom to share about running an organization and working with people. Much of what Clark knew of leadership he gained from this delightful old gentle man. By observing the way my husband treats older people, I have been the beneficiary of learning to be a better listener and recognizing that older folks still have much to teach us. As I've aged, I'm grateful for others who value the elderly---which is where I am now!

Clark even unconsciously mimicked his first boss. He sometimes would walk around jingling change in his pants pocket, just like Albert. It drove me crazy, but I figured out after meeting Albert that my fiancé had even emulated his mannerisms. To this day he still recalls Mr. Ice and can recite from memory a portion of a poem honoring his mentor (written by his hometown friend, Dennis Daly):

Never has there been a man with wisdom, age and grace
That helped so much the little man and lived up to his pace.
This single man with great expression, help, and great advice,
We speak of the one who leads us all… We speak of
Albert Ice.

From that first job with the Y, Clark began a career that always included honoring those who had gone before him. Dr. Hugh "Bucky" Brown helped Clark honor another such man. Dr. Brown, a local Chattanooga orthopedic surgeon, had strong affection for Camp Ocoee, the Y camp near the city. Clark was curious about this passion and decided to visit the camp with Bucky and find out "the rest of the story." Driving out to the camp was a delight. In almost any season the Chattanooga landscape had a beauty that made one appreciate being alive. The camp was nestled at the edge of the Smokey Mountains and although the cabins were rustic, being near nature and the pristine water was worth any discomfort. Dr. Brown, then in his 40s, seemed to light up as they drove down the familiar trail to camp. Bucky shared that he had no father figure at home, so camp director and founder, Mr. Glenn (Chick) Ellis, became his mentor. Bucky had gone out to camp for 10 years and treasured those growing life experiences and the dear Mr. Ellis. Clark decided to honor the old camp director and organized a 90th birthday gathering for Mr. Ellis. Many of the city's leaders drove out just to honor the man who it seems

Clark stands with his first boss, Albert Ice.

had raised them all. The founder of Camp Ocoee was a symbolic father to many who went on to become successful businessmen in the community.

I still recall the day---it was lovely, bright, and sunny. The crowd sat outside in the midst of the tranquil setting. There were a number of touching speeches and even a letter of congratulations from the President of the United States was presented to Mr. Ellis. I was surprised to see how easily Mr. Ellis dismissed this tribute, but clearly relished the kudos from his former campers. His unpretentious smile said it all; the old camp director was genuinely thankful that the Y took time to honor him.

In every city where he had a leadership role, besides former CEOs, Clark invited former board chairs and donors to major events. Each time he would acknowledge them and tout their service and leadership. He also never forgot to acknowledge the wives of these folks. More than once spouses would thank him for his thoughtfulness. By acknowledging those who have gone before you, you gain credibility in your thoughtfulness.

Clark says, "We stand on the shoulders of those who have gone before us, we must not forget them."

" I've learned that people will forget what you said, people will forget what you did, but people will never forget how you made them feel.

MAYA ANGELOU "

Clark considers sisters, Cathy Raglin and Lori Swann, two of his best.

SQUARING THE CORNERS

Do the Mundane With Care~ Ordinary will become Extraordinary

Like many men of his generation, Clark mowed lawns to earn money when he young. He was very efficient and quick; but he also took pride in his mowing. He worked to make sure that the corners of the lawn were perfectly squared. At each turn, he remembers that he had to line up the mower so that the next mown strip would slightly overlap the last. It was not easy under the hot, humid Indiana sun bearing down on the young gangly boy. Numerous folks noticed his attention to detail and hired this youngster. He made a nice cache of spending money throughout those summer months.

One lawn stood out: the one at the local Y. Knowing so many patrons from community came to this center daily, he wanted it to be picture-perfect. One day Y executive Albert Ice observed how with only a push mower, Clark worked to square the corners. Ice came out and said, "Son, if this is the way you work, as you get older and begin looking for a career, you will go far. You are taking pride in your work and it will reap benefits, I assure you."

Clark never forgot that moment. During his entire career if anything was amiss in any of the YMCAs under his watch he made sure it was corrected...even if he had to correct it himself. He never felt he was too good or too superior to do even the most humdrum tasks.

Lori Swann, CEO at Triangle2 Solutions, a nonprofit organization management company, shares a noteworthy story that occurred in Nashville in 1987 about another humdrum task---making coffee:

"My first experience with Clark taught me so much. I was young and arrogant. I had been employed at the Y nine months

and was just figuring out the lay of the land when a new leader was thrust upon me. I was fed up with the Y and, in my view, it's antiquated systems and sexist leaders. I was counting down the days until I had been there a year, could put it on my resume and get on with my life. Part of my exit plan included getting a graduate degree, and with my boss' permission I came to work at 5:00 am every day and left at 2:00 pm to take classes. So, I'm at my desk working in my preferred undisturbed state when I first met the man that was arguably the most influential person ever in my professional career.

Enter Clark David Baker, anxious, eager, eternal morning person . . . and nothing would ever be the same.

Clark, 'Can you make the coffee?'

Me, 'I don't drink coffee so I don't make coffee,'

Clark, 'That makes perfect sense, but can you help me figure out how to make it because I really need some.'

Me Unspoken: 'I'm in – I love to be needed, but I'm keeping my attitude.'

I was an assistant to an assistant to an assistant, but Clark valued me, asked my opinion and listened to my ideas (and you know I had a lot.). When I suggested they move me to Green Hills to be a membership director because youth sports had 1/8 the revenue of membership and they had a youth sports director but no membership director, he made it happen.

When I published my first newsletter he called me and couldn't have been more excited if I had secured a $1 million gift. When I hit my monthly sales goals he congratulated me. When I 'wowed' him with my membership retention plans, he obliged by being 'wowed.' When a few years later I applied for a branch exec job he supported me. When he realized he would be out of the country on Y business when the decision was made, he didn't get on the plane without leaving two letters for me: one for if I got the job; one if I did not. That's unconditional love. The decision of where my path would lead was out of his control, but the fact *that I was a valued member of his team was not. I was loved and valued whatever happened.*

I got the job. Wow -- Branch Exec of the Brentwood YMCA. My first day on the job we opened at 5:00 am, so I got there at 4:00 am and sat in the parking lot until the opener, Jim, arrived. I introduced myself, and then offered, 'I'm here to help, what can I do?'

Jim answered without a blink, 'Can you make the coffee?'

And that day my past flashed before me and I laughed, but I wanted to cry, too, because I understood for the first time what Clark's leadership meant: your importance has nothing to do with the task you are assigned, it's about the significance of the task and how you fulfill it. Making coffee for the morning crew at the Y is as significant as it gets. I had the opportunity years earlier to show my servant leadership skills to the CEO and had failed. This time I was ready...thank you, Clark."

Lori became one of his top executives and a very close friend. Her creative skills, attention to detail, and commitment to mission made it easy for Clark to promote her to executive positions.

Making a point to do even the routine well may have been pressed on his mind even more by a board member who set out with him early in his Nashville tenure to visit Ys. Entrepreneur and well respected Nashville leader Nelson Andrews was also a pilot and loved his helicopter. Wanting my husband to experience the central Tennessee topography and view some of the centers from the air, Nelson offered to fly Clark to visit a number of Y's in the area that could accommodate a helicopter landing. Clark had alerted the specific centers and suggested they would be landing on one of their sports fields, specifically in the center. Upon arrival at the first Y, he was a little off center of the chalk line which he determined would be his landing point. Clark teasingly said, "Nelson, you just missed your mark."

Guess what? Nelson made no comment BUT every other landing, Clark noted that the pilot made sure he was precisely on the mark. Nelson took the routine of landing on a mark and made it a point to perfect his skill and proceeded to land the copter as if it were the bullseye on a target.

As they toured, Clark told Nelson to notice anything that should be improved. Afterwards he would appreciate sharing feedback---corrections would be made, if necessary. After the first Y tour, Nelson said very little.

"Nelson, did you see anything amiss or note any needed changes?" Clark asked.

"Well, I did see a few things, but you know, it's *just* the Y."

Internally, Clark was embarrassed---what did Nelson mean? Just because it's the Y, does that mean it's acceptable to be less than the best? My husband still recalls that day and has made every effort to make any YMCA he was responsible for, the very best---in appearance and in quality programs. Just as Nelson corrected his helicopter landings, Clark wanted to make sure his organization was something to be proud of and was determined to make the YMCA exceptional.

Growing and improving must always include education. My husband continually wanted to learn so that he could keep on top of the current trends. He used to say, "CEO does not mean Career Education Over." He attended and participated in regional meetings and national conferences, always in a quest to absorb more information and knowledge to improve and hone his skills. I used to attend a number of the conferences and acquired knowledge that helped me grow as a person and in my career field of education.

For example, both Clark and I never tired of attending Jerry Panas' workshops on philanthropy. We always took at least one nugget of information gleaned from the guru of fundraising (In 2016, Philanthropy Media announced their "America's Top 25 Fundraising Experts" and Jerry was number ONE!).

Even during tough times Clark made sure his staff was able to attend trainings/conferences that would improve the quality of their work. Continuing to learn may seem like something mundane, but it can make an organization a step above others who tend to ignore and not foster an individual's growth and knowledge.

Today, in any YMCA where Clark has been the CEO, the Y has earned great respect and admiration from the community each serves. Even though he has retired, if he sees a piece of trash on the floor or a picture askew at a Y, he will dispose of the trash or straighten the picture. Details make a difference. And it all started with that little boy who used to "square the corners."

Perfection consists not in doing extraordinary things, but in doing ordinary things extraordinarily well.
ANGELIQUE ARNAULD

Newspaper ad announcing the new aquatic center- 1975.
This was Clark's first fundraising campaign.

DECEMBER MIRACLE MAN
Relationships are More Important Then Task

"Clark, I've dug a lot of holes, but none has meant more than this Y project."

This proclamation was made by Washington, Indiana, philanthropist and oil company executive Henry Gwaltney when the local YMCA opened the city's first indoor swimming pool in 1975.

When Clark become the executive director of the Washington Y in 1973, he soon realized the facility needed an indoor pool and locker rooms to serve the community. He also realized that only a capital campaign could produce the necessary funding---and his campaign consultant, Bill Kemp, told him he would succeed only with Henry on board.

Fortunately, Henry was already one of Clark's great friends and mentors. This early relationship proved to be invaluable to the tiny YMCA that my husband loved so much.

Each December Henry would call the young executive and ask how the year was going. If it was a tight year, the philanthropist wrote checks to help the Y balance. In fact, everybody at the center called Henry "Our Christmas Miracle."

It's critical to have the right person lead a capital campaign. Henry's success with Gwaltney Drilling Company and Midwest Natural Gas confirmed his financial capacity. Added to his strong support of the Y, Clark knew this was his key volunteer to raise $600,000. Henry agreed to chair the campaign, the largest the town had ever undertaken.

As the effort unfolded, the Y began receiving numerous surprising pledges from businesses with which the center had no history of giving. Clark laughed at one such pledge from an egg company---he knew of no one involved

Clark checks out the construction of the new pool.

with the Y that was connected to eggs! He discovered later that Henry had been a silent investor in many small businesses including banks and farms such as Eggs, Inc. This man quietly bankrolled many of these companies when they were established or were in trouble; therefore, when Henry asked various owners to contribute to the capital drive, they gave. The December Miracle Man came through again. The campaign was a huge success. As the $600,000 campaign neared its goal, Henry expressed his deep satisfaction to the young executive. His strong relationship with Henry proved to be valuable in helping to build an indoor pool that is still benefitting old and young today.

Another example where relationships are more important than task comes from Gina Petersen, former executive director of the Brenda and John Duncan YMCA in Houston, Texas, when Clark was CEO. Gina is now working at the Y national headquarters.

"In March {2013} my brother was tragically murdered out of the country. Our family was devastated and then to add insult to injury, he did not have life insurance so there was no money to get his body home. Clark heard about my circumstance from some of the other senior leadership. He contacted me to let me know that the YMCA would be donating money to my brother's fund. The donation was almost a third of what we needed. I was overwhelmed by Clark's generosity. Being able to not worry so much about the money allowed us to focus on the grieving process. There is not a day that goes by that I don't think about what Clark and the YMCA have done for me.

Last year, a dear friend lost her job (so did her husband) within a few months of being diagnosed with stage two breast cancer. I did a fundraiser at my house to raise money for their medical bills and other expenses. Clark donated money out of his personal account to help. Because of him and other generous donations, we raised over $10,000.

These events have made an even stronger urge for me to help my fellow YMCA employees when they are struggling. We currently have a young staff person who has been in the hospital for over three weeks. Our staff team has come together to donate money to help her with her bills since she hasn't worked in a month.

It is truly a pay it forward example!"

Besides building strong relationships with board members and donors, my husband worked to build relationships with staff members. Lori Swann worked with Clark in Nashville and shares one of her favorite things about him that resulted from building a positive rapport:

"Clark can confront. I made a mistake and told my sister something that was confidential and she told someone…and you

know the rest. When Clark confronted me on it, I was embar-
rassed and crushed, but I was reminded of the saying, 'this hurts
me more than it hurts you.' I learned the importance of confiden-
tiality even more because he showed me his heart."

Since Clark officially retired and we returned to Nashville, he still sees benefits from relationships built over
time. He has felt fulfilled by consulting part-time for the
Nashville Y, renewing old acquaintances, and meeting new
staff and volunteers who had come on board since his departure.

Former staff member, Kathy Raglin, had her heart set
on completing a special project at the Robertson Y in Nashville before her promotion to district executive. It was to
secure funds for a commercial kitchen which would help
feed children at a nearby group home. It was a huge undertaking that fell short by $50,000.

Just before she officially moved to her new position,
Kathy phoned along with local philanthropist Jackie Guthrie. I could hear Clark speaking excitedly when he answered the conference call: "What?! Jackie, that just about
brings me to tears. I can't believe this! It will mean so much
to the Y and this means so much for you to say those kind
words. Thank you for calling me personally to share to
good news!"

"What was that all about?" I inquired.

"Jackie Guthrie told me that she had just made a
$50,000 gift to help complete Kathy's project! Isn't that
wonderful? She had to call and share this gift as she blames
me for getting her involved in the Y so many years ago.
Jackie told me that I started it all. That's pretty overwhelming for an ole guy from a little town in Indiana. It sure
warms my heart."

One key reason Clark has been a successful leader is
that he truly values relationships. Relationships with staff,
relationships with board members, and relationships with

Y members have all taken precedence over tasks. From the moment he stepped into a new position his focus was on connecting with the community. He seemed to know everyone---I struggled sometimes connecting the right person with what part they played in the community, but Clark knew them well, including the type of car each drove!
 I especially loved that he spent time getting to know everyone in his Y---from the sweet lady who folded towels in the locker room to the maintenance man to the instructor who taught aerobics. Yes, he spent plenty of time with his peers and executive staff, but he never forgot those who were not in the top leadership. Clark knew the importance of relationships and how they can make employees want to come to work everyday and embrace their mission.

Jesus said, 'Greater things of these you shall do...' Become a peace builder, a bridge builder, not a destroyer, and the way you do that is through friendships and relationships, and through authentic character.

RAVI ZACHARIAS

Clark is determined to climb the pole at camp in front of donors.

Clark is greeted with silly string at a Y welcome.

THE GREAT GOLDFISH DIVE
Learn to Laugh at Yourself

The 1973 capital campaign was a success and the pristine brand-new indoor swimming pool, named in honor of major donor Henry Gwaltney, was ready to be christened in Washington, Indiana. Clark was quite excited about the unveiling. His plan was to kick off opening week of the pool by hosting an overnight party for the children of the community with fun pool games. One activity would be called "Diving for Dollars." He threw 25 or so silver dollars in the pool after which the children dove in and retrieved the silver treasures. This was fun and worked quite well.

The highlight of the evening, however, was what the young director thought was his most creative idea: The Great Goldfish Dive! As children excitedly waited to plunge in, Clark released hundreds of goldfish into the pool, allowing the children with plastic baggies to catch as many of the little golden fish as possible. Prizes were awarded for the most goldfish caught, ranging from simple small fish bowls to the top prize of a lovely aquarium complete with colored rocks and a plastic diver inside blowing bubbles. The children were exuberant as they left the overnight event with their new pets. Some children had already named their fish and couldn't wait to share the news to parents that there would be a new addition to the family.

As the event clean-up began, Clark noticed that not all the fish had been caught and those few left were floating on top of the water and of more concern, they were dead! Their previous gold luster had turned to white.

Then the calls began-----parents complaining that their children's goldfish were no longer alive. Clark did not realize that chlorine kills fish---no Google back then. The First Place winner's mother was particularly upset as she had a lovely large aquarium with floating lifeless fish and a child who was upset because his new pets were dead. Feeling dreadful about the entire incident, the young program director dashed to his car and drove to the adjacent city (he had depleted the fish supply in his hometown) where he purchased fresh fish to replace the expired ones.

It was a lesson he's repeated to many: do your homework when introducing a new activity.

Another humorous incident had occurred in 1971 when Clark was day camp director in his hometown. The weather that day was rainy with the gloomy forecast to continue. The young director had played games and led the children in various activities, but his bag of tricks was getting low and he was running out of ideas.

What could he do? He decided to take his small group of about fifteen campers to the Dairy Queen to treat them to five-cent ice cream cones. Because he didn't want 15 kids running awry outside the fast food establishment, Clark thought he would just go through the drive-thru. The children were excited as he drove up in his Y minivan, ready to order. Suddenly, as the van began to proceed under the overhang, there was a jarring jolt and everything stopped! Clark had hit the overhang. His van was higher than the drive-thru height. Embarrassed, but calm, he painstakingly backed out, parked, and went in to buy the ice cream cones himself. He didn't hurt the building, but he did hurt his pride. He will tell you that he did what he had to do--when he ran into an obstacle, he made lemonade out of a lemon.

Another funny situation in 1985 brought my spouse much ribbing among his peers.

My husband glanced out the window as his plane taxied down the runway in Chattanooga, Tennessee. As the CEO of the Chattanooga Y, he was headed to Cleveland, Ohio, for a national meeting. Looking forward to a cup of coffee and reading the paper he had grabbed in the airport, he took in a deep breath and closed his eyes momentarily while half listening to an announcement from the flight attendant.

"Fasten your seat belts for our two-hour flight to Minneapolis."

"What?" Clark almost jumped out of his seatbelt, "I'm going to Cleveland, NOT Minneapolis!" The announcement startled this now clearly misplaced traveler. Clark nervously stopped the attendant who told him there was little she could do at that time.

How did this happen? In those days, security was far less intense and Clark was focused on the meeting he was to attend. He had been up early to catch the plane, and he also had to change planes in St. Louis before he landed in his final destination, Cleveland. After a short snooze in the airport, he just boarded the plane at his gate. Unbeknownst to him, however, Clark had slept through a gate change, obviously undetected by flight personnel; he was on the wrong plane!

So on to Minneapolis he flew, from where he hopped on the next available flight to Cleveland, his original destination. Yes, he was late.

He garnered a good deal of ribbing from his peers when his gaffe was uncovered. Clark did not want anyone to know about his blooper as he was embarrassed, but he did call a Y friend before he left Minneapolis. That friend got quite a chuckle and promptly shared Clark's blunder. By the time he made it to the meeting, it seemed as if the entire world knew.

After hearing of his experience, one attentive person learned a valuable lesson even though she was quite young when my husband told this story.

Elyse "Sissy" Phillips Hopkins (Clark's mentor's daughter) shared how that story impacted her, *"I learned to always check my ticket and gate number before entering the plane. I also listen carefully to announcements and not to fall asleep in an airport while on a trip!"*

Clark has always had a wonderful way to make fun of himself. When he shared stories about mistakes in his career, there was a lesson he was trying to convey. He found that by telling a story about himself and not embarrassing anyone else who made a similar misjudgment, then his staff would "get the point" without calling someone out. In most all of those situations, his employees learned from Clark's self-deprecation and improvements were made.

Another young friend, Rebecca Gallo, also noted Clark's penchant for getting lost.

"Clark was the first person I ever knew to have a GPS. I remember hearing so many stories about how much he got lost over the years. I learned to know your weaknesses and don't be afraid to take the help that is available to overcome them."

Laurie Bricker, former metro Houston

Clark having fun at a Y meeting.

board member relayed this: *"At every annual meeting, Clark would be the star of the presentation to the audience. He didn't win an Oscar or Emmy, but he was definitely memorable and kept us laughing! Clark's legacy with the YMCA will be one of vision, expertise, leadership---and lots of humor. He has changed our Y's in Houston forever with his magical touch."*

 To make mistakes is human; to stumble is commonplace; to be able to laugh at yourself is maturity.
WILLIAM ARTHUR WARD

CEO Bill Phillips taught Clark his most memorable lesson in decorum.

CHEWING GUM ENCOUNTER
Pay Attention to Dress and Decorum

It was a typical Monday morning executive meeting. Orlando CEO Bill Phillips had routine meetings with his top executives to discuss and share happenings in the Y.

This particular morning one young executive decided to pop a piece of gum---a breath mint of sorts. He sat through the meeting taking notes, chewing and enjoying the minty taste. As Bill dismissed the team, he asked Clark to remain. This happened occasionally as the CEO's office was located in the center where my spouse was the executive director. Bill many times had suggestions or concerns with the building and Clark, always wanting to please, would take mental notes on any issues needing to be addressed.

"Clark," Bill began, "I feel you have a future in the Y. You have all the attributes of a good leader. So, everything I share with you, know that I'm wanting you to excel."

Clark began to wiggle in his seat. Where in the world was he going with this comment? His budget was on target, the building was clean, the members were happy…

"You sat in this meeting, chewing gum, and looked like a cow chewing his cud. It's not professional. Don't EVER come to one of my meetings chewing gum again," said Bill.

"Yes, sir. No problem. Thanks for sharing," Clark meekly replied.

He did not see that coming! A simple thing like chewing gum was bothering his mentor, something so minuscule as chewing gum. Yet, he knew Bill was right, little things can make a difference.

Clark never chewed gum at the office again. He has used that story numerous times to give as an example of how important it is to look professional if you want to move up in an organization.

In 1973, three years after his return from serving in the military, my husband was named executive director of his hometown Y in Washington, Indiana. Before his stint in the US Army and for three years after his return, he had been the program director at the center and knew 95 percent of the community. Clark made an effort to always spend money in town in order to support the local businesses. After our marriage in 1972, I moved to be with my husband and settled into the cozy small town atmosphere. I particularly loved a sweet classy woman's store---The Wardrobe. Owners Steve and Mary Jane Wirtz were personal friends. Clark shopped at the men's store adjacent to The Wardrobe. The salespeople there constantly tried to persuade my husband to buy the "latest" fashion…and many times there were successful.

Two items come to mind that Clark now wishes he'd never purchased. One, was a maroon man's jumpsuit. It

was early in our married life and I didn't want to hurt the poor guy's feelings, but it looked ridiculous. He wore it very few times, especially after he was pumping gas one day. A woman thought he was an attendant (truly the one-piece did resemble a mainte-nance uniform) and asked if he'd check her tires. The sec-ond was a polyester maroon and white checked blazer. I used to tease Clark that he looked like the comedian, Pinky Lee, a children's TV show host in the 1950s. Wearing a bowtie with the blazer added to my husbands "over the top" Pinky Lee appearance...not exactly a professional look. But it was the 1970's and that style was "in." Worst of all, Clark was so proud of this blazer that he wore it to the grand opening of their new pool. Photos from the event still hang in the lobby of that Y. Clark has threatened to bring a nice blue marker and color over the blazer, wishing now more than ever that he had chosen something more inconspicuous. Perhaps he should have used his marker in this news article taken in 1974---take a look at those pants!

When we moved to Chattanooga, Tennessee, from Orlando in 1976, Clark learned another lesson in decorum. In Florida, he dressed as the "natives" dressed. And in the "Sunshine State" wearing bright colors was popular. My husband had array of pants that varied from bright green to white to khaki. I recall one pair of corduroy pants, in keeping with the preppy era, had ducks embroidered all over. He also had some interesting shoes----like his white saddle oxfords.

Chattanooga was a friendly, lovely city, but more conservative than Orlando.

A 40-TON CRANE lifts T-beams into place on the building site of the Gwaltney Aquatic Center as Henry Gwaltney, associate chairman of Action '73, Charles T. Rose, general contractor, and Clark Baker, executive director of the YMCA inspect building plans. Sections of the aluminum pool will be delivered in October and assembled at the site. The building is set for an early 1975 opening according to Baker.
(Times-Herald Photo by Greg Thomas)

Clark wishes now he'd never worn the plaid pants to the local newspaper's photo shoot in Washinton, Indiana.

53

My spouse found out soon that it would be wise to adapt to the local culture. His board chair was Spencer Wright, who owned a company based both in England and Chattanooga. He was a good man, but no nonsense and very particular. Clark learned much from Spencer and it began soon after his arrival. The two met for lunch one sunny day at the Mountain City Club which was Spencer's favorite place to dine. Clark felt honored to have been invited and took extra time to select what he considered to be a perfect outfit from his wardrobe. Clark donned one of his favorites, feeling quite dapper in his summer attire---bright green pants, white oxfords, a crisp white polo, and his ever-ready blue blazer. He and Mr. Wright had a pleasant lunch discussing upcoming projects. Upon time to leave, Spencer commented, "By the way, where did you get those green pants and shoes?"

Clark and CEO Bill Phillips in Orlando, Florida.

"Oh, I bought them in Florida where they are all the rage," said Clark.

"Well, son," Spencer slowly responded, "You're not in Florida anymore."

Clark politely thanked him, came home that evening, and promptly sent the pants and the shoes to Goodwill.

Clark has passed on what he garnered to his staff. On

one occasion Clark invited one of his center executives to join him at a hospital gala. He was a promising young man who had recently been promoted and Clark wanted him to meet physicians and hospital staff who frequented the Y where he had just been assigned. Every man there was dressed in dark suits---a few even wore tuxedos. This young executive walked in wearing a long-sleeved shirt---no tie, no jacket. Although no one made a comment, it was clear he had dressed inappropriately. I felt uncomfortable for him, but it didn't seem to bother him in the least.

Clark said nothing that evening, but the next day this young lad had an email indicating that he should never get caught wearing a casual outfit in a formal setting. He then suggested always having a blue blazer in his car---just in case. In this day of "casual Fridays" (which are looking more like casual Monday-Friday) I feel sure the young man didn't think it was important to "dress up." BUT he got the message and thanked Clark for his email.

Today if you were to peruse Clark's closet, you would mostly see khaki, blue or grey slacks and a plethora of blue blazers. He learned that in his line of work, those colors will serve you well. You will not see one pair of green slacks!

> **Good manners are important in all aspects your life, including what you choose to wear. Knowing the proper attire for every occasion can make the difference between success or failure, both socially and in your professional life.**
>
> ## DEBBY MAYNE
> ## ETIQUETTE EXPERT

The Y is all about children, so children were involved in many YMCA celebrations.

PARTY FOR A WHITE CADILLAC
Celebrate Anything

Everyone in Chattanooga recognized Catherine Helm's old 1979 four-door white Cadillac DeVille. She would joke about her old car while her peers were buying the latest styles. But Catherine loved her white car, and it ran just fine. She never suspected this car would play a key role in honoring her.

Catherine was known for her volunteer work in Chattanooga, particularly at the Y. She had the southern charisma that could charm a tiger. Not only did the she serve on the executive board of the Chattanooga Y, but she also served on the Blue Ridge Assembly Board, the South Field YMCA Committee, and eventually the National Y board. Clark wanted to celebrate her giving spirit in some special way. He decided to host a surprise birthday party for her white Cadillac. The car was turning 10 years old, and Catherine had kidded about this milestone numerous times.

The date was set and many of her friends arrived for a special lunch. Catherine thought it was a gathering to celebrate the very successful reading program that she helped establish and staff.

One of the staff offered to "park" her car while she was at lunch. The Cadillac was then taken to be detailed, washed, and waxed. A huge bouquet of flowers was placed prominently on the hood of the car.

Lunch was held at the downtown Y, which had its own catering kitchen. After enjoying delightful dining with friends and staff, Clark said, "Catherine, I have a little surprise for you. Come with me."

She walked out the front door, followed by the entire group, where her old car had been strategically parked, glistening in the bright sun. Catherine could not believe her eyes! Sitting there ready for its driver was her white Cadillac looking as fresh as a daisy with this beautiful arrangement.

Clark and Catherine share a light moment.

She was astonished and grateful for such thoughtfulness. Her infectious laughter and bright smile of gratitude said it all. It had, indeed, been a fantastic way to honor this special volunteer.

Clark always found special ways to show his staff, his donors, and his board how grateful he was for their service and/or their gifts. He felt it im-

portant to celebrate and create a fun place of work, or in the case of board members, a fun place to volunteer. He knew people worked hard for the Y so he believed they deserved to play hard---the two were intertwined (with the addition of prayer).

Clark told me that regardless of who you are or how much you're worth, there's always room for a t-shirt, a balloon, or notes from children to brighten your day. He purchased a helium

tank in order to have balloons "on call," ready for any occasion. The marquee in front of each facility was a great place to announce birthdays and congratulations. If a board or staff member had a baby, he sent a cute bib along with a Y-logo onesie to the newborn with several brightly colored blue or pink balloons...an unexpected treat for new parents.

On one occasion, the Y team even decorated a plane. Nashville Board chair, Margaret Maddox's husband Dan needed to fly to Houston in order to have a pacemaker implanted. Clark wanted to find a way to show the Maddox family that the Y was thinking of them during this time. His communications director, Julie Sistrunk, found a creative way to decorate their small private plane. Clark and Julie met them at the airport to wish them well. Julie had arrived early so she could decorate the plane with balloons and a banner. She had also placed good luck and best wishes cards on the seats inside the aircraft that were handmade by the after school daycare children. She knew the couple would enjoy reading the cards to pass the time while in-flight. Julie took a photo of Dan proudly wearing his YMCA sweatshirt before they stepped into the plane. It truly meant the world to him and Margaret.

My husband was amazed at how little it took to make someone happy. Celebrating even the tiniest apparently insignificant events can boost the morale of your entire organization.

Clark presents board member, Florence Davis, with a birthday surprise cake.

The more you praise and celebrate your life,
the more there is in life to celebrate.

OPRAH WINFREY

Clark with Nashville Dominican Sisters at Camp Widjiwagan

Clark and Carolyn with the Vietnamese Dominican Sisters from Houston.

THE DAY THE "C" WENT OUT AT THE Y
Pray Together, Have a Belief

The Chattanooga downtown Y was a city landmark. It was a stately, well-built structure. From the expressway one could see the giant letters Y-M-C-A prominently featured on top of the building in huge neon lights. I always loved seeing it as I drove toward our home on Signal Mountain after working out and picking up the girls from the Y's after school care. It was a wonderful reminder of a place where my husband worked and where, as CEO, he truly could do so much for so many folks---young and old.

One day the lights in the "C" went out because of a simple electrical issue of some sort. I recall that the downtown Y began to receive call after call asking, "WHY is the "C" out of the YMCA sign?." People wanted to protest if the Y was removing Christian from the organization's name. On other occasions the "Y", the "M" and the "A" had gone out and little was said, BUT when the "C" went out, the citizens of this little city let their voices be heard!

Clark told all those he spoke to that under his watch, the "C" would never go out. The unlit "C" letter was taken care of the very next day with all the letters shining tall and proud overlooking the lovely river city.

For anyone who knows Clark, there would never be a question of preserving the "C" in a YMCA where he worked. His faith has always been of utmost importance in both his personal and professional life. His Chattanooga board chair and national YMCA board member Catherine Helms said it this way:

"When Clark was in Chattanooga, we became good friends. He taught me the real meaning of the "C" in the YMCA and the amazing scope of the organization...from child care to new camp programs to scholarships to renewed emphasis on our Christian

63

mission, Clark led us with thoughtful enthusiasm. He is creative and practical. These two traits have enabled him to be a success in all of his work. He has kept us ever mindful of our Creator as we have joined him on his YMCA journey."

My husband loves mornings—he works out sometimes as early 5:00 am. His runs (now it's a walk) include reflection, meditation, and prayer. I have no doubt that each morning he prayed for each Y under his watch as well as for his family and friends. His close relationship with the Dominican Sisters (in Nashville and Houston), as well as the Sisters of Providence who taught him, are important friendships to this day. I always tell the sisters that I feel he owes part of his success for their constant prayers for him.

Clark firmly believes that the Nashville Y resident camp came about via the power of prayer. This is story he told me:

"Among one of the most wonderful things I was able to do in my 50 years with the Y is to have been a part of creating the Joe C. Davis YMCA Outdoor Center, aka Camp Widjiwagan. In 1994 we were blessed to have the Corps of U.S. Army Engineers lease us this camp for $1 a year for 300 years! In those early years, there was much controversy on the property, who was going to use it, and what it would do to the area. I asked the Dominican sisters of Nashville to pray for our not-yet-built-camp.

We fought hard, some staff (Tom Looby and Julie Sistrunk) were told at one community meeting to "shut up and sit down" as they defended our usage. We needed donors, so we got a houseboat and I brought 20 board members out to see the site from the water. Since some of them were wealthy Nashville business folks, the rumor started that we were going to build condos there for the rich and famous.

One Sunday morning, we had set up a call between entrepreneurs Dan and Margaret Maddox and Congressman Robert Clement. When the call was going on (we had it on speaker phone), the congressman asked how many kids might be on that

350 acres at one time. We actually didn't know, but made up a number…and Dan told them, about one kid an acre. Then the question about cars/traffic came up….and Mr. Maddox said, "Congressman, I don't think many 10 year olds drive to camp, we'll use a bus."

Dan wore him down….and in the end, we won on a summary judgement from Judge Thomas Aquinas Higgins, who is named in honor of the famous Dominican Saint, is a patron of the Sisters. The judge is still around, and loves the Dominicans. Since I could not really do anything for him, I wrote him a note one day and said in honor of your support of our camp by giving us the judgement to proceed, we'll invite the Sisters to come out and use the property once we are in business. I have never forgotten that promise and the sisters continue to enjoy the camp each year."

Fast forward 5 years to 1999, Camp Widjiwagan was growing and very successful. The Y had a capital campaign to build cabins to make it an official residence camp. A donor offered to give the Y $5 million IF and only if they could raise a matching amount by December 31st of that year. Camp Director Mark Weller called Clark. My husband knew what to do---he requested prayers from the Dominican sisters again and all 150 of them fervently began to pray for a match. Mark thought it was a "hail Mary pass" as it appeared they wouldn't be able to raise the funds. BUT voila, they raised the money for the matching gift. We believe it was with the help of the sisters' petitions to a higher power that this miracle money came through.

Since that time, the Dominican Nashville sisters come out to camp (young ones in the fall and older sisters in the spring) for a day of fun and recreation. Clark and I send a check to help cover some of the costs, but since the sisters literally prayed the camp to this point, the Y staff members are happy to host them.

Louis Paine, former board chair of the Houston Y wrote, *"A close companion of Clark's through most of his Christian life was the book, My Utmost For His Highest. This book was based upon devotional talks by Oswald Chambers while serving with the YMCA in Egypt with Australian and New Zealand troops who were guarding the Suez Canal during World War I. Clark has expressed his gratitude to God for all he has accomplished. The leadership ability he has shown requires preparation and more preparation. Clark can truly say 'I am here for God to send me where He will.'"*

Faith is not a light which scatters all our darkness, but a lamp which guides our steps in the night and suffices for the journey.

POPE FRANCIS

Colleague and friend, Gene Dooley, with the Bakers.

A MEETING WITH TACKY SIGNS

Pay Attention to Little Things

No Gum Allowed
STAFF NOT ALLOWED TO USE THIS PHONE
Please use other door
Meeting of building committee postponed
Checks or cash only please
PLEASE SHUT DOOR QUIETLY
SEE FRONT DESK IF YOU HAVE TROUBLE WITH YOUR CARD

The above are all examples of handwritten sloppy signs that were randomly taped to walls and doors with scotch or duct tape that Clark collected as he traveled from one facility to another after arriving in Nashville in 1994 as CEO. His favorite was a sign posted near the basketball goal that read: NO DUNKING. You can only imagine that this sign tempted players to do the opposite: more dunking!

Clark prominently taped each and every sign he collected (there were enough signs to fill one entire wall) to the walls at his first meeting which included all of the center executives. So that no one would feel "left out" or no staff would sense that they were being "picked on," he made sure every facility was represented. Every Y had this "sign disease".

"Ladies and Gentlemen, what you see before you is a compilation of various notes/signs I found while visiting each of your YMCAs," he began. "These look shoddy and unprofessional. Not only that, a mark is often left from the tape when you remove the sign that is challenging to take off. I don't want to ever see another sign placed like this. If you need something posted, have it professionally created and put it up properly. People notice the little things...dirty bathrooms, dust on floors, sticky gym equipment, unkempt employees, and yes, even tacky signs. Regardless how wonderful your programs might be, if your facility is not cared for, you will neither retain members nor grow your membership. We are a first class organization and I intend for us to have the finest reputation in Nashville, which, by the way, will help to further our mission."

Tacky signs disappeared. After that meeting, Clark rarely saw a sign that was posted improperly. If he did, he removed it and gave it to the front desk, sending a clear message.

Perhaps it was an idiosyncrasy, but Clark wanted the Y centers to be clean, crisp, and welcoming always. He felt that way about our home. I tended to let things pile up and address the matter later, which frustrated him. (I'm sure he shared this story with me hoping that I would follow suit. I'm much better today after having lived with this man for over 42 years). Clark firmly believes that by paying attention to the little things, people will immediately assume your product or service is above average. Your reputation will grow, your business will be a success.

Carole Carter, former district executive director for the YMCA of Middle Tennessee, wrote this email to note much of what he taught her about leadership and attention to detail:

"Sam Stephens the Operations Executive for Green Hills told me that Clark was stopping by. I told him to take good care of him…make sure staff are not chewing gum, keep the weeds out of the mulch, always be prepared to offer a prayer, a navy blazer will do you well, if you are charging up the mountain, you better turn around and make sure someone is following you, make sure to say thank you more than you so please…"

Former board chair Catherine Helms from Chattanooga shared this humorous story about paying attention to little things. I enjoyed her story, but am happy that the spraying didn't asphyxiate the board!

"Once, on the day of our Metropolitan Board meeting, there was Clark spraying the room with Mountain Breeze air spray. He explained that the chairman had noted that the room had a peculiar odor. Clark was doing what Clark does best. He was doing something about the problem. It was a small thing but one I will never forget for it showed me how important it is to DO something about a problem. I would have smiled in agreement, but never would have sprayed the room! He did what needed to be done. This aspect of Clark's personality is why Chattanooga had so many innovative programs under Clark's leadership."

How much attention should be allotted to orderliness and cleanliness? A whole heap…it's an ongoing undertaking. Not only that, but what every person perceives as clean or neat can be quite different. When Gene Dooley, a good friend of ours and CEO of a large Y, came to Nashville in 1995, he offered to visit a few Ys, noting any issues that might need attention. He told my husband that he would be like "a secret shopper" as no one knew him. Clark thought this would be beneficial, but with one caveat. He called each Y and warned them that someone might be coming to check out their facility and staff. Encouraging them to spruce up the place and have everyone be at their best, Clark just knew he would get a glowing report. Shockingly his friend returned with four legal pad pages filled with lists of items that he found needed addressing. His friend's father had been a protocol officer in the service so this man learned from a young age to pay attention to details. After that experience my husband realized that one can never be too clean---there's always something that can be improved.

As an executive becomes immersed in the daily issues of his/her organization, it's easy to lose focus. When he first arrived in Orlando in 1976 as executive of the Downtown Y, my husband pulled up in his car, parked, and made notes of all he saw outside the Y that needed "attending to." He saw a plethora of Floridian florae, shrubs, and trees that clearly needed pruning, gravel that had been flung outside its proper area, and tiny bits of trash absentmindedly tossed by passersby. Clark gathered the maintenance crew and the clean-up began with this exec helping out to demonstrate to staff the value he placed on having a spotless facility inside and out.

Fast forward a year later. Clark pulled up to park and sat perusing the outside of the building. Guess what? The flora was overgrown, the gravel was scattered, and trash was once again strewn about. Clark recognized that with all the other issues of keeping a facility and staff running smoothly he had lost focus and missed the details. He realized that as he told me, "You can't let up."

To create something exceptional,
your mindset must be relentlessly
focused on the smallest detail.
GIORGIO ARMANI,
DESIGNER

Nashville Dominican Sister Mary Angela displaying her CLARK BAR.

THE FAMOUS CLARK BAR
Communicate, Communicate, Communicate

It was simple really...a thin white jewelry box lined with cotton, tied neatly with ribbon and three helium balloons (Four caused the gift to "take flight."). Inside the box was a Clark candy bar. The CEO gave them out on various occasions. It could be anything from a welcome gift, to a "you've done a good job" message, to birthday greetings, or as treats given at the end of a presentation. One thing I noticed was that they were very valued. One staff member told me that she had seen the candy bar presented many times but had herself never garnered a Clark bar. He noted the omission and rest assured she had one the following day. One recipient had hers framed and placed prominently on her office wall. It was Clark's special way to communicate that he valued that person and wanted to acknowledge it in some special way. My husband firmly believes that he is keeping the NECCO candy bar company in business with his ongoing purchases of his "Clark" bars.

Most often the candy bar was accompanied by a note of congratulations or a thank you. It was heartfelt and communicated a true sense of caring and telling that person, "I value you."

Paula Gavin, former CEO of the New York YMCA said: *"When I saw Clark distribute this candy bar to others, it taught me three things about leadership:*
1. Being kind to others is a motivator to do more.
2. Recognizing people is an inspiration to strive to do better.
3. Using your own name connects you and promotes your commitment to developing others."

"Clark bars" were only one of the ways my husband communicated effectively. His handwritten notes seemed

At his retirement, The Nashville Y presented Clark with this neon Clark sign with his favorite saying.

to come at just the right time for many of his staff, although his hand-writing is challenging to read at times. Scott Charlesworth who worked for Clark during those early years shares a communication he still holds dear:

"It was June 1978. Clark and the Central Florida YMCA were very instrumental in me being tapped for a YMCA international assignment in Papua, New Guinea. It had been a couple of years in the making but finally I was preparing to leave Orlando and head off to the South Pacific.

I remember it was late afternoon and I had stopped by my office to pick up a few things and head to town. Among the things that I had grabbed was an envelope addressed to me in Clark's handwriting. While I was driving down Dillard Street I could not get that letter out of my mind. So I pulled to the side of the road, opened the envelope and found one of the most thoughtful, sincere and supportive messages that, to this day, still stirs my emotions. None of this should have been surprising, of course, as Clark was a close friend by then and he had been encouraging me throughout the application process. However, to see in black and white his sincere expression of excitement, joy and respect for me was extremely powerful -- and a message that I would draw upon for years to come.

As a leader in any endeavor supporting one's staff is critical and for Clark, and me as well, it is also the source of much joy. It is not a fringe activity or 'management technique' but rather something at the core of why we do what we do. And, as such, I have tried to regularly express support to those with whom I have worked and care about as well. So what's the big deal? Why do I refer to that moment in time so far back in my own career?

Isn't supporting junior staff part of 'Management 101' or just plain common sense? Well, actually no -- not for everyone I have learned. So to receive Clark's message that day was a real gift to me: A gift not only of friendship but of leadership. The real power of such communication is the realization that as a leader (whether a peer, a supervisor, or a CEO) we are provided with a unique opportunity to impact the lives of others, perhaps well beyond what we might have ever imagined.

It's been over 35 years since I read that note and I have tried never to lose sight of this responsibility and opportunity to help form others along the way. I rarely collect keepsakes. However I still have that letter written in 1978 that I so gratefully received on that June afternoon."

Elizabeth Dubuque, a former employee and retired COO of the Florida Suncoast Y wrote this about Clark:

"If there is one thing that stands out for me it is that he wrote me so many notes and letters...from the shortest...glad you are joining our team, etc. to a few longer letters/emails expressing his gratitude for my work, counsel, enthusiasm, friendship, etc. AND I kept them all! I re-read them last Friday and smiled. I am quite sure I was not the best employee Clark ever had but he made me feel I was...I am sure most of his former/current staff feel that same way and I know many volunteers do as well. He is so good at thanking people and showing appreciation...it is a gift he has and the mark of great leader."

66 **A lesson I learned from Clark was his strong belief in personal, handwritten notes to donors, members and friends. I have done my best since to follow his lead and believe in that somewhat lost art of communication. Clark has inspired so many, and I am glad to be counted amongst those.**

JOHN C. ALEXANDER, RESOURCE DIRECTOR, ASSOCIATION RESOURCES, YMCA OF THE USA **99**

When Clark became CEO in Nashville, Lori Swann and Julie Sistrunk became two of his most valued staff members.

ONLY TWO THINGS WILL GET YOU IN TROUBLE

Spend Time on Talent

It was in the dining room of Ingram Industry, one of the largest companies in Nashville, where Clark received one of the best pieces of advice to become a successful leader. He and Board Chair Lee Barfield visited Ingram's Senior Executive Officer Phil Pfeffer. Lee had suggested a meeting with Phil and other successful leaders who had a keen grasp of the state of the community. The Nashville YMCA was growing, but Clark didn't know if it had the capacity to keep growing. Lee asked some probing questions. What do we need to be watching for? What would he suggest as a way to be successful to keep up with the city's development?

Phil said, "There are only two things that will get you in trouble---you will run out of money or you'll run out of talent. If you spend your time on the talent, you'll never run out of money. Spend your time on talent and the money will come."

"Spend your time on talent," Clark repeated this in his head many times after that encounter. He never forgot that those words of wisdom from Phil and began, from that time forward, taking more time to recruit the best. And not just the best, but he sought out people who had passion. He ended up with a group of young, ambitious, bright staff members in Nashville who were ready for the challenge…the challenge of growing the Y during an unprecedented time in this flourishing city. The key was to keep up quality while having vision and funds to do so.

Lori Swan, Tom Looby, Bob Ecklund, and Julie Sistrunk became a strong team who were eager and willing to go full steam ahead. Lori, Tom, and Bob were operation vice-presidents, with Julie leading marketing and development.

Clark had coaxed Tom to come from Atlanta, hearing he was a bright, rising star. CEOs joked at conventions and meetings that they didn't like seeing their staff members talking with Clark for fear he would recruit them. That was true as my spouse was always on the prowl for the best and brightest. If there was interest in someone he would "court" them, using all the persuasive skills he could muster. Many of his colleagues chided him saying, "Baker, stay away from my staff, I want to keep them!"

Once I inquired why he was spending so much time looking for strong
prospective hires, he smiled at me and quipped, "You can't make up in training what you screwed up in hiring."

I particularly recall that Clark wanted a young man, Dan Dummermuth, in Nashville. We invited him and his

Dan Dummermuth–CEO, Mid-TN YMCA, with Clark

wife, Gwen, to Music City. Before dinner Clark asked for my help, "Carolyn, I really want this guy. He would be such an asset to our team. Let's do all we can to encourage them to come to Nashville."

The recruitment worked and Dan didn't let Clark down. He became the executive of a brand new center in Franklin, Tennessee. Under his leadership, it became a thriving Y and a real focal point in the growing community. My husband was so right about the young leader --- years later he has returned to become the CEO of the YMCA of Middle Tennessee.

His wife, Gwen, still recalls how Clark sent her flowers when she first arrived. It meant so much to feel welcomed, especially during the first days when arriving in a new city.

One day Clark lamented to Nelson Andrews (one of the city's leaders) that this group was so eager that he had to "hold them down."

Nelson said, "Clark, you've got a great group of lions out there. And you need and are being paid to be the lion tamer."

While Clark occasionally had to call his team together to "make sure they were all on the same page" he allowed his talented, vivacious group of "lions" to go with their ambitions and desires. They had so many wonderful ideas and were always willing to work hard to produce the results. I do believe Nelson was advising that you need not "break" an excited, energetic staff by too many restrictions or shoot down their ideas as they will leave you. By being in the center of the ring watching and supporting, the lion tamer will have more success.

It worked. Nashville became one the fastest growing YMCAs in the country in the 1990s.

My husband was so proud of his team and all of their hard work. In my opinion, Clark didn't need to "tame" anything----they liked and respected their leader. Plus they flourished after seeing the positive results of their hard work in the city. Because of their lion-like aggressive enthusiasm this YMCA grew to new heights. My spouse recognized in those early years as an executive how recruiting bright, talented staff made all the difference.

Operations VP in Nashville, Lori Swann wrote, *"Clark builds awesome teams. He believes in building the best team possible, made up of the best in their fields, even if they aren't his best friends. One of my favorite quotes from him: 'I love that everyone of you are smarter than me. If you aren't, then why do I need you?'"*

Clark even took time to advise young leaders when he was on vacation. Mike Van Haelewyn, now senior director in the international division of YUSA in Chicago, is an example. We first heard about Mike when he worked in high school as a summer life guard at my parents' recreation center in Hurt, Virginia. Mike credits Clark for helping him select the Y as a career when he was young:

"While I enjoyed being a member and a part-time employee at the YMCA, I never really gave it serious consideration as a career option. However, my parents were wiser than I – and clearly saw that I might have a future in a non-profit organization. One day, they pulled me aside and suggested I talk with Clark Baker when he came into town. My parents told me that Clark was the CEO of the YMCA of Middle Tennessee and that he might be able to offer some perspective on finding a career.

Soon after, Clark and Carolyn came back to my hometown near Gretna, Virginia, for another family affair. Ruth Simpson made a point of introducing me one Sunday after church. Clark was kind, jovial and completely down to earth. He asked me questions that were genuine, sincere and relevant to my interests and my limited YMCA work experience. I was young, still in university, and really had no idea of what my career interests or trajectory were at the time; yet Clark spoke to me in a way that validated my stage in life, gave me subtle ideas to consider, and permitted me to take risks and seek adventure as I pursued a career path.

My understanding of the YMCA as a movement was narrow at best – with the Altavista Y being the gold-standard of operations. Little did I know that I was talking to an icon of the YMCA movement, and to the CEO of one of the largest YMCAs in the nation.

I always appreciated that conversation and note that as one of the defining moments in my choice to pursue the Y as a career. Clark's humility and ability to 'meet me where I was' is indicative of him as a leader: someone who understands human relations and can motivate action by helping an individual discover their own selves. At that moment in time, Clark was the YMCA personified: an organization that gently nurtures and empowers the community by listening, guiding and inspiring."

Spending time on talent didn't mean just recruiting employees. It went far beyond that. As someone once told Clark, "Feed your staff or they eat your members." It's so true. If your employees are not happy they won't do their best and it will be reflected in how they treat others and perform their job.

Today, it's called "empathy" and a number of companies are focusing on empathy as a new strategy. On the front page of the Business and Tech. section of the June 22, 2016, The Wall Street Journal, is an entire article that focuses on empathy training. It states, "Individuals who master listening and responding to others are the most successful leaders, and this skill outranks all others, concluded a study released this year by Development Dimensions International. The finding reflects assessments of more than 15,000 leaders in 18 countries. About 20% of U.S. employers offer empathy training as part of management development…"

Clark started out as an empathetic leader. He continually tried to be present to staff, balancing their emotional well-being, while being sure they were doing a good job. He was there to listen to problems or advise them if they confided in him. In meetings he worked diligently to share the importance of attitude and the way they treated others in the Y---peers, volunteers, and members. Laurie Bricker, former Houston board member, wrote:

"As a board member, I noticed the attitude of staff at every level. I remember asking him if his Y directors went through some kind of presentation training, as he regularly invited them to board meetings to update us---their personalities and enthusiasm were contagious, and a reflection on Clark's approach to mentoring and building confidence and leadership in each of them."

Former chief financial officer (CFO) of the Nashville Y, Bart Bartleson, wrote this about Clark's leadership style:

"Clark Baker always impressed me with his unwavering confidence in the people around him - friends, family, staff, and volunteers. He always allows people to bloom by not blocking their sun light and letting them and their dreams stand tall for all to see…From the first day I knew Clark 'had my back' and he infused confidence in me to do the best I could for the Y."

One of most touching stories to share how Clark nurtured his staff comes from Patricia Osborne, director of youth development, of the Houston YMCA.

"Soon after Clark moved to Houston I experienced some of the darkest days of my life. The days and nights were very long for me and I found myself fighting for the emotional well-being of my children and also trying to understand why Mike was sick and why God found it necessary to take him from us when we were so young. Many days I cried the entire one hour drive to work but always when I got to work I would find people who cared and supported me. For that I am forever grateful to the YMCA of Greater Houston.

One particular day when I got to my office I had a note from Clark laying by the telephone with the 'thoughts in solitude'

84

prayer. It meant a lot to me for him to take the time to let me know that he knew I was going through a rough time... when I thought he did not even know who I was. Many times over the years I have noticed that it is the little things in life that set Clark a part from others. The smile in the hallway. The kind hello at the door. Words in an email letting us know that he knows we work hard......words letting us know that we are doing well."

M Y LORD GOD, I have no idea where I am going. I do not see the road ahead of me. I cannot know for certain where it will end. Nor do I really know myself, and the fact that I think that I am following your will does not mean that I am actually doing so. But I believe that the desire to please you does in fact please you. And I hope I have that desire in all that I am doing. I hope that I will never do anything apart from that desire. And I know that if I do this you will lead me by the right road though I may know nothing about it. Therefore will I trust you always though I may seem to be lost and in the shadow of death. I will not fear, for you are ever with me, and you will never leave me to face my perils alone. +++

THOMAS MERTON
— Thoughts in Solitude

 The most important task a CEO does is recruiting, hiring, training, and retaining.

CLARK D. BAKER

Clark congratulates Christin on her first official run. The both ran together in Orlando, Florida.

Clark with daughter Christin after receiving the 2016 Humanics Award from Springfield College.

SOMETIMES A PROGRAM DOESN'T MAKE MONEY

It's All About the Mission

"*I was a junior in high school, 17, and let me tell you I had things figured out,*" writes Clark's eldest daughter. Christin sheds light on mission better than anyone I know.

"*I had earned my first real paycheck the previous summer as a lifeguard at a Y pool. I was taking a business/political science class in my high school. I felt I could really talk to my father as a budding CEO and tell him a few things about how to run a successful Y program. I mean my class had just won the Junior Achievement stock contest! The one where your class purchases fake stock and then after six weeks you see if you made money or lost money on your picks. I had taken the lead in helping our class pick---I think mostly because I really was the only one interested. We won against all the high schools in the Nashville area and received a plaque. I fancied myself a budding investor at the time. I would grab the stock page of the paper and look up my stocks each day and track them. I had a head for business, my 17-year-old mind told me, and was going to be a successful business woman.*

It was a Saturday afternoon and my father and I were at the Brentwood YMCA in Nashville. It was the weekend before youth soccer started up and we were walking around the fields. I can't remember why it was just the two of us, but I remember really feeling like we were colleagues, me and my mind for business and

Daughter, Caroline, playing at the Y.

my successful father CEO. I felt like an adult and very important surveying "our fields." My father was telling me about this program. The Brentwood Y had one of the largest youth soccer programs in the YMCA of Middle Tennessee, that year they were going to have 1,700 participants enrolled. I remember being very impressed with that number. They were lining the fields as the two of us walked around and you could see the little flags that marked each corner. I was asking my dad a few questions about the program, why it was so large, was it the biggest in the nation, how much money it made, you know- those business things adults talk about.

As we were heading back to the parking lot my dad told me, 'This program loses money each year.' I was floored. This program loses money? They have 1,700 participants? It was by every measure I could figure successful. This was not a good business model---how could my very successful father allow something like this to happen?

'If it loses money each year then why do you run the program?' I asked.

'Sometimes you don't run programs to make money; you run them because they impact lives,' he replied.

There it was.

I was silent.

I forgot. I forgot what organization my dad worked for.

I got so caught up in my quest for business acumen, in my search for stock prices going up and things that make money. I forgot what really matters… making an impact on people. That's the business model of the Y and I forgot. My interest in business started to wane after that and I was off discovering another potential career choice- news broadcaster.

Years later when I was the Membership Director of a YMCA in Durham, North Carolina, we did a cost study. It was then that I understood that most programs in the Y, when given the burden of square footage, salaries, lights and operating expenses, lose money (except for membership, which helps cover everything).

Clark proposed across from the Heidelberg Castle in Germany---1970.

My brother-in-law, Allan Lavoie and my sister, Dianna, stand next to Clark in Vienna, Austria--1969.

Carolyn and Clark were married in 1972.

Carolyn's sister, Dianna, and the Baker's daughters held a surprise 40th anniversary gathering at Longwood University where they were married.

Celebrating 30th wedding anniversary at the beach.

Baker family photo taken while living in Orlando, Florida.

Lifetime friends of the Bakers, Tina Harr and Cindy Fergason, met when they worked for Clark in Orlando.

Clark learned much from these Chattanooga, Tennessee leaders. Shown here Left to Right are John Guerry, Spencer Wright, visiting CEO of the YMCA Of the USA, Solon Cousins, Raymond Witt, and Chattanooga Y CEO, Clark Baker.

Family photo taken when the Bakers lived in Chattanooga, Tennessee.

Clark with daughters Christin and Caroline. The commitment to mission trickled down to family.

Life long work-out buddies in Nashville.

Family photo taken at the dedication of the Clark D. Baker Lodge, Joe C. Davis Center, Nashville, Tennessee.

Paddles given out at the dedication of the Clark D. Baker Lodge, YMCA Joe C. Davis Center,

The Bakers having fun at the rodeo in Houston, Texas. Clark's last assignment was at the Y in Houston before his retirement.

Larry Kellner, one of Clark's most dynamic board chairs in Houston, is introduced at an annual dinner gala.

Ribbon cutting ceremony at the dedication of the Carolyn and Clark Baker Science and Arts Center at YMCA Camp Cullen, Houston. Philanthropist John Duncan views the moment the Bakers cut the ribbon.

"Camper Clark" was given out during the dedication of the newly reconstructed YMCA Camp Cullen in Houston.

As I was sitting listening to the consultant roll out the numbers I remembered my walk across the soccer field with my father and I heard him say 'You run them because they impact lives.'"

Clark's commitment to the YMCA mission was evident from the time we met when he was serving in the United States Army. Oh my goodness, this guy loved the Y and spoke fondly about it incessantly. I figured if marriage was "in the cards" with this man he would be working for the Y his entire career. Fifty years later, I know I was right. His passion never floundered. The mission was first and foremost in his mind. If asked about the Y mission, he quickly spouted forth, "The Y mission is to put Christian values into practice through programs that build healthy spirit, mind, and body for all."

Clark always reminded me and others that the Y was NOT an organization of Christians, BUT a CHRISTIAN organization. He felt strongly that helping others in any way should take top priority.

Perhaps one of the most impressive examples of a

 mission statement in practice was Operation Backpack. Clark had heard that the Y in Richmond, Virginia, had successfully collected backpacks and school supplies for students of families who could not afford that expense.

As Houston CEO, he could imagine how inadequate those children felt who did not have proper supplies when returning to school. In 2005 he hired a new chaplain courtesy of entrepreneur David Weekly who wanted the Christian emphasis more prominently featured. Clark suggested

Operation Backpack to the chaplain who agreed and ran with the idea. It was a good way to put Christian principles into practice while giving children who had no supplies a positive beginning to the school year. In early August boxes were placed in each branch where folks could buy supplies and backpacks and conveniently drop them. Staff also accepted financial contributions for supplies. That first year the Houston Y distributed 35,000 backpacks filled with necessary school supplies to needy children. At the 10-yearmark, more than 345,000 children had been served. The chaplain found that other organizations were eager to partner and the collaborations with local news and radio stations plus Texas grocery chain HEB allowed the program to rapidly expand, helping far more children than they had ever dreamed.

Robie Wayne, retired senior vice president of the Minneapolis YMCA, speaks admiringly about Clark's attention to mission:

"Just this year (2013), as a volunteer I contacted Clark via email and requested support for the Sioux YMCA, the only Native American YMCA in the country. Within minutes he responded that it would be his pleasure to support the work on the reservation. His dedication and commitment to the YMCA can only be surpassed by his genuine caring for others especially those less fortunate. I truly believe that Clark is one of those rare individuals that every morning in his life wakes up and wonders what he can do for others".

 Outstanding people have one thing in common: An absolute sense of mission.

ZIG ZIGLAR

Celebrating the ground breaking of the Carolyn and Clark Baker Science
and Art Center at Camp Cullen with my favorite Texas storyteller, Y board
member, and friend, John Duncan.

Clark with board members Jimmy Webb and Bill Wilson.

A MILLION DOLLAR VAN
There is no Mission Without Money

If you are not 100 percent believing in what your organization is doing, QUIT and do something else. Your staff, your customers, and your donors can spot insincerity a mile away. Since I met my partner over 45 years ago, he has embraced this belief.

Clark believes in the Y mission, is passionate about the mission, and lives by the mission. His zeal was evident to everyone. The excitement in his voice and the hours he dedicated to his life's vocation were outward signs to all that he had a commitment to excellence using the Y as a platform to help people improve in body, mind, and spirit.

Even with this strong belief, Clark realized from the moment he was hired by the Y in the small town of Washington, Indiana, that you cannot support the mission without money.

When we first arrived in Nashville in 1987 Clark took time to visit all the board members. Realizing there were great needs, but no appetite for fund raising, he commissioned well-respected fundraising consultant Jerold Panas to conduct a feasibility study on the Ys capacity to raise money in the community. Clark valued his expertise and was eager to hear the results from the 60 leaders and philanthropists Jerry had interviewed to assess future fundraising capacity. Clark met with Jerry before he was to report his findings to the board.

"We only need a few minutes---it won't take long," Jerry reported.

Curious about that comment, Clark was not sure he wanted to hear negative findings especially since he was just beginning his tenure in Music City.

Jerry's findings were simple and straightforward: "Everyone loves the Y, but no one could tell me why."

That's the moment my husband realized that he had to educate the public about the mission of the Y and share all the good this non-profit was accomplishing through outreach: especially helping underprivileged youth in Nashville who seemed to have nothing and had no guidance in their lives. Every community in which we lived had issues that the Y helped to address. From settling refugees, to helping women recover after breast cancer, to offering daycare for single mothers trying to finish high school---the list is endless. Clark knew that educating people was the key to securing their contributions.

In Nashville, Tennessee, a unique way was discovered to share the mission. After the board became aware of the need to educate donors about the Y's work, they understood and agreed with the young CEO. Finding a way to enlighten potential donors and community leaders would inspire this philanthropic community.

Three board leaders, Bill Wilson, Jimmy Webb, and Margaret Maddox had the ingenious idea of taking potential givers on short "awareness" tours. Clark concurred and suggested that a new "conversion" van would be perfect. They could set up short tours of various Y programs and facilities that were doing work for the underprivileged kids and do so in a comfortable setting. However, the board did not sense the need for a new vehicle, leaving him to use the old, worn out 12-passenger minivan. Clark took that "lemon" and made "lemonade." He purchased a new van himself! It became our family car. It was a state-of-the-art van for that time, it had all the upgrades with a TV/Video-tape player (boy, did our daughters love that), soft comfy seats, and an upgraded sound system. He was ready for the next step—inviting and getting donors to take time out of their busy schedules to take a tour.

With the help of Bill, Margaret and the staff, meticulously planned tours began, always including Clark in addition to one or two board members. The tours took place around noon to respect donor's valuable time. Staff served tasty box lunches while riders watched an impressive video about various programs of the Y as the van took each group to two or three points of interest. Donors learned what could be done if more funds were available. The volunteers toured facilities, met with young people, and were even able to speak with a number of parents who were grateful for the positive effect the Y was having on their kids. No one was asked to contribute during the tours as this was simply done to make donors aware of the programs and good works of the YMCA. The tour helped volunteers become keenly aware of the breadth of service the Y was doing for the entire community.

One such stop was the group home where young boys who had been in trouble were placed after leaving juvenile jail. Sometimes one or two young men spoke to the group about what the Y had done for them, providing a path to changing their lives for the good.

On one particular tour, the van stopped at a basketball court where the Y performed outreach work in a disadvantaged neighborhood. Although the dilapidated courts needed repair, staff played games with the children who were there. One benefactor was so touched he wrote a check that very day so courts could be improved.

The van began regular tours, reaping unbelievable benefits. Most people had not realized the depth of the Y's reach, especially for the poor. The money began to roll in and the pledges were impressive. The vehicle became known as the "million dollar van." The triumphal achievements of the tours were largely due to the combination of enlightened donors, committed board members, AND, at the helm, an enthusiastic, effervescent leader who clearly had passion---a strong belief in the mission.

Other leaders in the Y movement recalled Clark and his attention to mission. Howard Mezile, retired CEO of the Minneapolis YMCA, relates this:

"When I worked for YUSA (National Y headquarters) I went to Nashville to do consulting work for Clark. I watched Clark present a motivational talk to inspire his staff to improve financial results. He is an exceptional inspirational leader and speaker. A quotation stuck with me throughout my career. Today, 'no money, no mission' is a prominent and often quoted saying across our movement, from coast to coast. Clark has a special ability to capture key ideas in simple phrases."

If you have a belief in what you are doing, if you are committed, and if you are passionate, this will be evidence enough for people and they will respond positively.

Your million dollar van might be a million dollar slide show; a million dollar speaker, a million dollar program. Whatever it is success will not come unless you believe in your mission; however, there will be no mission without the money.

Never doubt that a small group of
thoughtful, committed citizens can
change the world; indeed, it's the
only thing that ever has.

MARGARET MEAD

Board chair, David Schendeldecker, and Clark "ready for flight"
at a Houston annual meeting.

CLARK'S BEST FRIENDS
Connect With Board Members

The evening honoring Nashville volunteers was packed. The gathering was always fun. Staff had worked diligently to prepare a special event to thank many good folks who volunteered all year long. It was climaxed by handing the gavel over to the next board chair. An honor to be sure....this is when Clark switched allegiances in a humorous way.

Volunteers from all over the Nashville area came to celebrate and recognize people who had given many hours of their valuable time to help at the Y or who had donated money for the myriad of projects in which the various Ys played a part.

With the deep desire to show his appreciation Clark tagged this one event as the single most celebrated day of the Y year. The theme this particular evening was Hollywood. Volunteers were made to feel like they were celebrities the moment they walked down the sidewalk outside the event venue...walking a red carpet with bulbs flashing, photographers galore (Y staff) shooting photos of the guests. Mixed in were "look alike" celebrities. Donors and volunteers had a ball having their pictures made with them. (I recall having my picture made with look-alike Garth Brooks). Tables were adorned with glitter and stars. The stage looked like a page out of the Academy Awards.

Clark made sure the metropolitan board had tables closest to the stage; his staff knew who they were and many were assigned to greet and direct them to their tables. The evening included ever popular performances by some of the children involved in YMCA activities.

After the Volunteer of the Year from each Y received his or her award, Clark came forward to announce the "changing of the guard." He bragged about the past chair, Sandra Fulton, thanking her for volunteering time and service.

"And now, ladies and gentlemen," he said with gusto, "I'd like to introduce you to your next board chair AND my new best friend, Bill Turner."

The entire audience laughed loudly and applauded, because Clark had begun naming "Best Friends" since he arrived in Nashville. Everyone knew how he played on this phrase and simply loved the chiding. His first "Best Friends" in Nashville were Ridley Wills and Bill Wilson. Ridley had chaired the search to bring Clark to Nashville, so he felt particularly indebted to this good man. Bill was his first board chair--Bill wanted Clark in Nashville since they first met when Clark was CEO in Chattanooga.

The positive response from calling board chairs his best friends encouraged him to continue adding best friends even when he transitioned to Houston, Texas.

There was more than meets the eye to the term "best friend" in the context of the Y board chair. What Clark meant to imply was that he would do whatever the chair requested and it was assumed that the two of them would become very close as they would be spending a good deal of time together during the chair's tenure.

That was the tip of the iceberg on connecting to board members. Clark wanted the cream of the crop, the leaders of the city, and other influential people to be a part of the board. He did everything he could to make this board THE board to be on.....I believe he succeeded in all the cities where he served.

Why was my husband able to get such stellar folks to become members of the Y board?

Bill Wilson said it best, *"People would ask me why I worked so hard as a board member and I told them that Clark made it fun. We had goals, but he made it fun."* He also told me that

Clark with one of his favorite "best friends" Bill Wilson.

he knew no one who could work with a board better than
Clark.

Other reasons that Bill noted were:

• *We just had to show up and all was done. Clark made volunteering easy. I recall how he was steely focused and somewhat stressed whenever he had board meetings. He wanted
them to be perfect. They were well run, started on time, and
rarely, if ever, went overtime. Tables were decorated, food was
enticing, and emphasis in recent years was on healthy lunches. Everyone who spoke knew there was a time limit. Clark
realized each board member's valuable time was being given to
the Y and he swore to never abuse it.*

• *Bill liked that there were no surprises. Clark had everything
very organized and if he told a board he'd do something, he
did. His comment, "I never had to worry about anything."*

• *Clark communicated so well. He knew his board and if he saw or read something he thought a particular board member might enjoy, he sent a note or email with an attached article or photo. He kept the board up to date on Y matters and news.*

Yes, Clark worked hard to get to know his board. I recall an occasion in Houston when my husband was invited to throw out the first pitch at the Houston Astro's major league baseball game. This ceremonial tribute (usually reserved for celebrities, executives of companies who contribute to the team, or community leaders) occurs at each home game. Rather than take the honor himself, Clark asked one of his board members if he would like to throw that pitch. Why that particular member? He had confided in Clark after a meeting that he was going through a divorce and it had been particularly difficult for his son. Clark also knew this man loved the Astros and might want to throwout this first ball along with his son. That board member was elated, and as my husband watched him and his son on the field being photographed with the one of major league players, Clark knew he had done the right thing. Later, the board member shared how much it had meant to him and especially to his son.

This attention to the importance of a board trickled down to our children. Our oldest daughter, Christin, had a humorous but honest take on her memories of Clark, his board, and the value he placed on that connection:

"I understood the importance of a board at a very early age. My father's first job as a CEO was in Chattanooga Tennessee, back then the title was still General Director. We moved there from Orlando Florida when I was going into the second grade which would have made me eight and my sister, Caroline, four. The whole family had just moved into our new house. We were getting settled and used to our very different surroundings.

The family was invited to a welcome party that was hosted by the board. This was the first time my father, the CEO (General

Director), was introducing his family to a very important group, and vice versa. My father really wanted my sister and me on our very best behavior. We were by no means unruly kids but we were young and unpredictable.

I will never forget being in the back seat of our 1982 station wagon with the faux wood side panel. Caroline and I were in matching dresses and patent-leather shoes. It was dark out so I couldn't see my father's face while he was talking but Caroline and I were very attentive because he was using a tone that he rarely used and we knew we should listen.

'Girls, I want you to be on your best behavior tonight. You say yes ma'am, no ma'am and yes sir and no sir. You look people in the eyes and give a firm handshake. These are my board members, they very important people, they can fire daddy.'

Caroline and I understood that our father was going to be 'the boss of everyone' and so I think he wanted to make sure we knew that there was a higher power out there and that higher power was his board. To a 4-year-old and 8-year-old there was nothing scarier than a parent being fired. Fired we understood more than death and getting our dad fired was the last thing we wanted to do. I don't know that my sister and I have ever been better behaved since that very first board gathering.

I looked everyone in the eyes, I shook their hands with an eight-year-old iron grip and said yes sirs and yes ma'am's like never before. Caroline was the best behaved 4-year-old in the world that evening.

Since then I attended many functions with my father's boards and it never fails that whenever I meet a board member I always hear my father's voice from all those years ago. 'These are very important people, they could fire daddy.'"

Houstonian Laurie Bricker wrote how she viewed Clark:

"I was fortunate to be a Y Association board member when we hired Clark as our CEO. My immediate impression of him was his fresh and open outlook on the YMCA and its potential *growing impact on our city. He had vision, leadership, respect for diversity and kindness. I once invited Clark to the Jewish Community Center to present to the JCC Board. He did so with such excitement that I remember thinking how envious the JCC was of the YMCA having Clark as our CEO! He has always been willing to share best practices---and admit ideas that didn't quite work out."*

Coming together is a beginning; keeping together is progress; working together is success.

HENRY FORD

Clark wanted a photo with Carolyn before he left for Arizona. He knew it would be an experience that would change his life forever.

THE INTERVENTION
Deal with Your Demons before they Deal with You

I could feel my heart pumping. I could sense the tension in my body accelerate as I walked over to the central office of the campus where I worked in Nashville. I had been coaching my forensics' team after school, preparing for the next speech competition. Someone came to be with my students as it was relayed this was important. I was told nothing else so my mind quickly went to the concern that there was an accident, someone in the family had gotten ill....I just didn't know. What could be so critical that I had to be escorted out of school during a time when I was in the middle of working with students? Our best friend David Snow walked me over and relieved my first concern---no, no one was sick or hurt.

Clark had begun his career in the YMCA working as a program director. He quickly was elevated to leadership positions with his first executive position in Washington, Indiana, at the very Y where he had been given a scholarship. Being a person who does not let any "grass grow under his feet" my husband began looking for other opportunities after he had finished a successful campaign for his hometown Y. He found that in Florida as associate executive of the Central Florida YMCA in Orlando. Six years later at the young age of 32, Clark became the chief executive officer (CEO) of the Chattanooga YMCA in Tennessee.

He would sometimes tell me, "I don't know how a little guy like me was blessed with running a Y of this size." Always successful, Clark worked extremely hard toward that end with intense exuberance---there was no stopping this guy. He loved the Y, he loved the mission, and everyone knew it.

With such a leadership position at an early age, there comes stress---big stress. The weight of making budget and carrying the mission was enormous. Clark reminded me often that there was no mission without money, and there was no money without the mission. The weight of the job and family and his past began to catch up with this young executive.

A priest once said that if you have any issues you've not dealt with as a child, they will come to haunt you in your 30s, 40s, or 50s. Clark had not dealt with a key issue that plagued him during his formative childhood years. Perhaps it was his gentle spirit that never wanted to find bad in anyone, perhaps it was embarrassment. Whatever it was, Clark could not admit that his issue was his mother---she was an alcoholic.

Clark never drank much---not even in college. As he quickly ascended the non-profit ladder, a drink here and there helped to ease the heavy burdens of being an executive and a family man. When he became CEO in Chattanooga, Tennessee, the drinking seemed to increase, however, it did not affect his job or family life. One time I discussed the increase in his drinking habits and Clark took notice. His drinking subsided.

It all changed, however, when he became the CEO of the Nashville YMCA. In 1987 this remarkable city was poised for growth and under Clark's leadership the Y began an unprecedented climb with new buildings and expansions in abundance. With all of the excitement and with a tremendously dedicated staff and board, Clark was feeling great, but the stress was mounting. He began drinking to get ready for events where he had to be "on." The drink or two helped ease tension. Steadily through the years the drinking would continue.

Eventually and unbeknownst to me, he began to drink at work occasionally. I NEVER thought that would occur.

I believe Clark thought no one noticed, but his closest staff and colleagues did, and they were worried about him. He was performing well; in fact, he was always receiving compliments and awards for his leadership skills. He thought that when he would put vodka in a diet coke no one would notice. And for awhile they didn't.

Two of his most dedicated staff knew something needed to be done. They feared for Clark's safety (yes, he did occasionally drink and drive) and they felt his performance level would diminish.

Seeking help, they confided in the board chair, who secretly met with a few other board members. With total devotion to this man who they all had come to love and respect, they knew something had to be done to help their leader.

Those caring staff and board members wanted any action taken to be private; especially because of the fear of this getting out publically. A psychologist in Nashville who works solely with high-profile individuals met with the small group and decided an intervention was necessary. They knew they wanted me on board.

The day I was summoned to the central office, I didn't know any of what had transpired---I was clueless.

I had noticed Clark was out-of-sorts at times, but attributed it to sugar issues since he was diabetic. Just before we stepped into the building, David hesitated, "Carolyn, I think it's about Clark and alcohol."

All kinds of emotions came rushing in---I was rightfully nervous as I entered the room. There was only one person in the room, Clark's friend and past board chair.

"Carolyn, Clark has a drinking problem," he said calmly. Knowing I might panic, he reassured me that it was not a big deal and that they were going to help him fix the problem and that he'd be as good as new.

At first, I tried to defend my husband.

"Are you SURE?" I questioned.

The past board chair told me that several staff had noticed and that there was enough proof that something must be done.

My head was swimming. "Listen, are you sure some staff might be angry with him and maybe they are exaggerating? Perhaps a disgruntled employee is trying to hurt his reputation. Clark has always wanted to be considered perfect in the eyes of his board. He would be devastated if he knew you thought any less of him."

I can't recall the exact words but his response went something like this, "Listen, Carolyn, the staff who shared this information love Clark very much. They just want to help. If you don't believe that your husband has a problem, go open his car trunk tonight. Open it. I guarantee you will find a bottle of vodka, probably half empty. We are going to have an intervention and get him help. We want you to be a part of this. If this is to be successful, we need you."

I looked into his eyes, wanting confirmation that I could believe him, trust him. It was all coming so fast.

"We need you, Carolyn. You cannot tell Clark anything. Call me tomorrow and we'll make arrangements."

A sick feeling deep inside came upon me. I left the room in shock.

Upon reflection, I had noticed that Clark usually came home and went to bed early. He seemed so stressed this past year. He never wanted to go out. He was becoming a recluse. I recalled asking him if he was alright and he admitted that he was stressed. I told him that if the job was too much he could find something else and we could move somewhere else, whatever would help.

"Your health is far more important than anything," I empathetically said.

Clark told me he would be fine. He just needed to get through this phase of fund raising.

The evening after the meeting with the board chair, I slipped outside to Clark's car.

In the dark I slowly opened the trunk, hoping that I would find nothing. There, tucked under a few old books was a bottle of vodka. I picked up the bottle, held it up, and in the moonlight, I could see that it was, indeed, half full. My heart sank. It was true. I wanted to walk in and confront my husband---how could he jeopardize his health, his family with this poison?

I didn't.

That moment was the tipping point. Realizing my husband, indeed, had a drinking problem, I needed to go along with whatever the board decided to do. I knew that if he didn't get help, he would lose his job, but more importantly, he would lose his life. Alcohol is deadly to a diabetic. I went into the house and called the board chair.

The intervention was to be kept confidential. Only a few board members and a few staff knew what would oc-cur. Everyone was determined to avoid discrediting Clark in any way. The psychologist, using his skills with high profile interventions, led the events that transpired.

This was a difficult time for me---I basically had to lie to my husband about the meetings I was attending to prepare to basically coerce him into getting help…not knowing how he might respond. This dedicated group wanted to get Clark the best treatment in the United States and found Sierra Tucson in Arizona. He would be asked to go for 30 days with the family coming the last week.

Telling our daughters, who are very close to their father, was not easy. Christin had graduated from college and was job hunting with plans to move to Los Angeles within months. When I sat down in our living room I told her the situation and the plan to get her father help.

"Good," she said, revealing that she had noticed her father was acting weird at times. She sensed something amiss, liked the plan and knowing that everything would be fine. Christin told me that she would be happy to write a letter and be a part of the intervention.

Caroline was more challenging. It was in her first year at Catholic University in Washington, DC, and she was enjoying college life; oblivious of what had transpired at home. She happened to be home for the weekend when I took her to dinner to disclose the family situation. Caroline broke down and cried, unable to finish her dinner. I reassured her things would be fine and that, even though her college schedule prohibited her from taking part in the intervention, I would keep her abreast of all that would transpire in the upcoming weeks. She returned to college hopeful and promising prayers.

The intervention was scheduled just before Thanksgiving break. That day in November, Clark was expecting a regular Y meeting at Margaret and Dan Maddox's office (Margaret was a former board chair and she and Clark had become fast friends).

Margaret felt too close to Clark to be a part of the meeting but provided the space. Margaret and Dan also offered to pay for Clark's treatment. When Margaret shared the situation, Dan said, "Margaret, is he worth it?'

Margaret didn't hesitate, "Yes, Dan, he is."

They also had their pilot ready to personally fly Clark to Tucson. Everyone in the room was nervous, but hopeful. When Clark walked in I knew he was shocked to see us, but he acted as if this was a nice surprise. The psychologist took charge.

Clark was asked to listen to each person and then later he could comment. One by one each person read or spoke to Clark. Sitting around the table were Clark's board chair, his pastor, his best friend, David Snow, his oldest daughter, Christin and me. Each of us read a letter basically sharing our love and admiration for Clark, but things had to change to help him with his problem. One of the most poignant moments was Christin's letter where she repeated several times "I want my father back."

At the end the psychologist shared what they wanted Clark to agree to---a 30-day program in Tucson, Arizona. He had been with the Nashville YMCA for 10 years and it could be touted as a sabbatical. No one need find out. His job was secure if he would take the suggestions.

We all held our breaths when Clark was finally allowed to speak.

"You are an answer to my prayers," he said. "I have been struggling about how to handle my situation and prayed for an answer. I can't thank you enough. If you don't mind, I'd like you all to join me in prayer."

We all stood holding hands and bowing our heads as Clark prayed. We all were amazed at his composure, almost too good to be real. The plane was ready at that moment and I had packed a bag for him, but Clark asked to wait until morning. He wanted to pack himself and speak to his staff.

David and I looked at each other----we were both nervous about letting Clark wait.

What if he changed his mind? What if he left town feeling embarrassed? After all, everyone in that room was special to him. Would he be so distraught that he might try something drastic? We decided that he wouldn't be left alone, but granted his wish. Immediately after the intervention, Clark and I drove over to where all of the center personnel were meeting. When the two staff who knew about the intervention saw Clark they looked at me, worried that the meeting had fallen apart. When I smiled and said that it had been successful, they both broke into tears.

Clark stood in front of his staff and spoke with such eloquence. Explaining that he had been with this Y for 10 years, and that he would be taking a break--- a 30- day sabbatical. The Y would be in good hands and he would continue checking in with them.

Later the priest who had been a part of the session told a close friend that the intervention was one of the most spiritual moments he had ever experienced.

So Clark repacked his bag that evening, emailed folks, spoke with board members close to him, and went to bed knowing he would be taking an extraordinary journey--- one that would change his life.

David Snow, the counselor, and Clark all flew together to Tucson in November 1997. David wanted to be with his friend for support. It was an exceptionally kind gesture.

Before leaving Clark secured a letter that was given to me which confirmed that his job was safe while he was in Tucson. He wanted his family to feel secure and supported. The board understood and was kind to write the letter.

Sierra Tucson was exactly what Clark needed. After his physical it was determined that he was what the Sierra team liked to call "vanilla" which meant that the alcohol had not hurt any of his major organs. They had caught his deadly disease before there were any serious issues. The days and weeks were good for Clark as he peeled away the onion, basically coming to realize that he had never acknowledged or dealt with his own mother's alcoholism. She had embarrassed him numerous times, but he kept it inside always accepting his mother's illness. That hidden part had eaten away at him all these years. Now, with the help of the treatment center, he was beginning to deal with his childhood. The 12-step program was the core of his treatment and it fit beautifully with the strong faith which he held.

Our youngest daughter, Caroline, and I came for the last week which happened to be during Christmas. We learned much about alcoholism and how each member of our family could help Clark in his journey to sobriety.

Dan and Margaret Maddox

Upon returning to Nashville he was welcomed as if he had been on a vacation. His gratitude was expressed via letters written to these extraordinary colleagues and volunteers who cared enough to save Clark's life.

Tragically, the month after Clark returned, his dear friends, Dan and Margaret Maddox, were killed in a boating accident. Had he not been to treatment, I'm not sure if Clark could have handled everything with such grace as he was asked to be one of the eulogists at their funeral.

It has been almost 20 years since that November "sabbatical". I am so proud of my husband who has never had a relapse thus far. Clark is grateful everyday for the gift of those caring staff and board members who took time, effort, and money to help a little guy from Indiana deal with his hidden demon.

❝ It's never too late to get help for any of your problems, and it can be done discreetly. What is even more important, you can be a successful leader if you deal with whatever problem might be hindering your job performance. Whatever they may be, "deal with the demons or they WILL deal with you".

COWBOY WISDOM

Clark D. Baker Lodge at the YMCA Joe C. Davis Center, Nashville.

YMCA Camp Widjiwagan water park, Nashville.

FROM PROTESTS TO "BEST CAMP AWARD"

Leading During Tough Times – Have a Plan

"We have an opportunity here." Clark would always say in reference to tough or crisis situations. One thing he knew for sure-- if he prepared for these occasions and thought them through with a plan in mind, the crisis could be resolved with minimal stress. I watched this myself numerous times and still smile when I recall how calm and unemotional he was---at least on the outside.

When he was CEO in Nashville, Clark and others had a vision for a first-class residential YMCA camp. They were fortunate to obtain a large tract of land from the Corps of Engineers on Percy Priest Lake. It included miles of shoreline, an idyllic setting for a camp.

Neighbors adjacent to the proposed camp, however, liked the land untouched and caused a stir and got the media involved. Ridley Wills, author and Nashville entrepreneur, wrote this about the situation:

"They 'went up in arms' about what the YMCA planned for the area. They began spreading rumors that the Y would be working with troubled youth and detention center kids on the property (fearing their quiet neighborhood would be disrupted). To combat this disinformation, Clark and board chair, Bill Wilson, met with editors of The Tennessean, the Nashville Banner, and local TV stations to discuss the details of our lease. 'In the end,' Clark said, 'We received hundreds of letters of support and only 17 in opposition.' Of course, Camp Widjiwagan went on to be a nationally-acclaimed success story, winning Nashville Parent Magazine's ""Best Camp Award" in its inaugural year and every year thereafter."

Camp Widjiwagan is part of the Joe C. Davis YMCA Outdoor Center named in honor of philanthropist, Joe C. Davis. The outdoor center includes the Nelson Andrews Leadership Center and the Clark D. Baker Lodge. It continues to be one of the top innovative camps in the country. In 2016 Camp Widjiwagan was featured in The Disney Way 3rd Edition as a "kids and guests first customer-centric organization."

Occasionally in Clark's career he ran across a few discontented employees who tended to bring a negative atmosphere to a particular Y. Clark knew he needed to deal personally with the negativity. Daughter Christin recalls it clearly:

"In the book 'Good to Great' by Jim Collins there is a section that talks about getting the right people on the bus or the right people in the right seats. I remember reading that section and having a memory from my childhood. It is weird when you realize a life lesson years after the actual lesson.

That book came out in 2001 and I was 26, but the first time I heard a great leader use a bus metaphor was when I was 15 years old and it was 1990--11 years before that book was published.

My father was picking me up from school but before we went home we had to stop by a meeting, he needed to talk to the staff. I went to a Catholic school so I was in my white button down shirt and khaki school skirt. The staff of the Downtown Nashville Y was gathered in the aerobics room. I was sitting on folded up mats near the door. I was told we would run in and run out and go home. As you can see my memory of this event is very clear, I didn't understand what was happening until 11 years later but I somehow knew I needed to remember this moment and that later it would make sense.

The staff sat on the floor of the aerobics room and my father pulled up a folding chair and sat on it to address the group, something he rarely did. He told the staff (I'm paraphrasing) that things were changing, roles were changing, and they now had different leadership and expectations. They may not like it and that's okay. This is the direction they are going and if they want to 'get off the bus" they can. And if they do, he and the Y would give them all the help they could to find a new place. If you're on the bus this is the direction it's going. Either you are on or off--- but it's your choice. My father also mentioned that the bus had a revolving door; I don't recall Jim Collin's bus having that.

I don't remember talking about the staff meeting when we left. I'd like to think I could tell that wasn't an easy thing my dad had just done and so I talked about something else. Really I think I was a selfish teenager and wanted to talk about some school event that had happened.

Since I have been in the Y I have been on many busses and I have gone through a lot of change. Some busses I have stayed on and some I have gotten off, but I've never been angry or resentful of the change that has happened. At the age of 26 that lesson I learned 11 years prior all made sense. Jim Collin's book just made me remember the lesson of Clark Baker.

- *I'm either on the bus or I'm not- it's my choice.*
- *I'm not going to change the direction by complaining.*
- *I just need to move on and get on a different bus.*
- *The CEO/board is driving.*
- *Y busses have revolving doors and some you get off and then you might want to get on again, so you better watch how you exit."*

Perhaps the toughest time of Clark's stellar career came while he was CEO in Houston. The budget in the growing Y went from $68mm to $110mm in an eight- year span. They had just raised the most money ever in their capital development program and in their annual Partners Campaign. They had committed to 13 capital projects including a new Downtown YMCA and had completed an aggressive strategic plan.

On September 13th of 2009 Hurricane Ike had a bull's eye on Houston and inflicted $15 billion in damages to the greater Houston area. Some Ys were closed for six weeks. The loss between child care and membership would exceed $3.5 million. An economic meltdown finally hit Houston and companies began to announce cuts, the housing market and oil prices both took a huge dip, and confidence began to wane. Add to this the swine flu— yes, this flu had an effect with camps and Y sports declining as many parents, fearful of their children catching the bug, wouldn't allow them to participate.

Clark and his leadership team had previously organized and expanded staff to support a $125 million organization over what they thought what be a huge growth spurt for the next three years. They were poised for the growth; they felt positive about thinking ahead and being prepared.

Then, just as suddenly as the recession hit, the Y revenue began to slow. Shockingly, the Y was heading toward significant losses each month. If left unchecked the Y would run its first deficit, default on their bonds, and lose the confidence of the board. When Clark was alerted to that devastating potential, he appointed a committee to study the situation that included his fiscal managers and some of his strongest board members, led by his board chair. The work in committee revealed that the revenue would hover in the $105 million range for the next two years at best, much lower than the earlier projection of $125 million. Leadership had already trimmed center operations staff and cut some $1 million the prior year. The committee decided that cuts had to be deep, swift, and at the top of the organization.

The criteria was simple: "what did we want vs what did we need?" The group decided they wanted to remain a strong, fiscally viable, YMCA that would not compromise the member experience.

The sad reality was the need to eliminate 17 staff positions---good people, strong people, career people, many friends, and all valued. The Y eliminated positions, dealt only with that, and implemented a generous severance program. This was nothing about the people, it was all about the ability to fund those positions. Clark ran this through more board people, to be sure they'd thought about everything. They did not want to eliminate or reduce benefits. They also tackled the supply chain, but 60 percent of costs were in personnel. That was the place to get the quickest results.

Once the decision was made, Clark began what turned out to be one of the saddest days in his 50-year career. He reminded himself that the financial health of the YMCA was his #1 priority, and that was the overriding thought that saw him through this process; but having to cut 17 positions devastated him. Many people were hurt, angry, disappointed in him…and Clark had to accept that. "Why me," was often the cry.

Through this dark time, Clark at times felt very alone. I was personally affected as my best friend in Texas was the wife of one of those whose position had to be eliminated. Clark had to break the news to me, too. I was very upset and unfortunately was not very sympathetic. The cuts hurt the entire family as both of us had spent many happy times with this couple. We both knew that after this occurrence, the friendship would be lost. It is in these times that knowing what must done hurts to the core of the human heart.

The Y ended that year right on the $105mm revenue that was projected. They did not cut benefits when many Ys across the nation did. They exceeded their annual campaign goal, raised an additional $7 million in capital, and learned to do more with less. Ironically staff giving to United Way and to the annual campaign grew by 9.5 percent. This revealed that those "still standing" wanted to show support, and Clark was proud to share this with the Metro

Board. Staff training requiring travel was not eliminated but was reduced. The Y's bankers, auditors, and largest donors were brought inside the Ys thought process. They sought advice and counsel from them. They met with major funders and shared the plan. While Clark was personally devastated, the Y leadership received high marks for the timing of the move, the depth of their cuts, and their willingness to spread the tasks over fewer senior people. Remaining staff were assured there would be no additional cuts. Neither did the Y cut inner-city programs; they were actually expanded, as well as the number of members receiving financial assistance.

When Clark retired in February of 2015 the Houston Y was right on budget, a million dollars better off than the previous year. Most of those who left found good or better jobs than they had before; membership units increased by a record 5,000, confirming the economy's slow come-back.

Faith and prayer was at the center of these moves.

Tellepsen YMCA, in the heart of downtown Houston, opened October 4, 2010

Every meeting began by asking God to walk with the group in this difficult journey. They made it through this tough time and were able to construct a gorgeous new Downtown YMCA and a new Houston Texans Y in the historic Third Ward—the first YMCA in the nation to be sponsored by an NFL team. In addition a new outdoor adventure center was

The Houston Texans YMCA is the first YMCA in the nation to be sponsored by an NFL team.

opened in the northern part of the city. After going through tough times, in 2010 the Y was able to joyfully celebrate its 125th year of service to Greater Houston.

 When in crisis, you need to assemble the best and brightest to help come up with an action plan. Then, regardless of the outcome, you must take the courageous steps that are needed to deal with the problem. And whatever you do, always do it first and foremost, with prayer, allowing that higher power to help see you through.

CLARK BAKER

Houston Y Development Director, Nanci Rutledge, with Clark and donors.

A $250,000 THANK YOU NOTE
Put Effort Into Friend Raising

His goal was to write seven thank you notes a day. Clark has always valued the handwritten note. Some recipients saved them for years-- one person had the letter by her bed, while another had it framed. One particular note made a strong impression, after a call on the Hamil Foundation in Houston, Texas. I interviewed one of Clark's development staff, Nanci Rutledge, who shared the following story.

Each year Clark and one of his staff visited the Hamil Foundation which funds youth, medical, and arts programs. Clark and Nanci described the Y's needs, specifically requesting scholarships for young campers who wish to attend Camp Cullen, but who could not afford to do so without financial aid. This organization funds youth, medical, and arts programs. The Y had been fortunate to be the recipient of a number of their grants; they especially embraced Camp Cullen. On this occasion Nanci joined her CEO for the annual appointment. After the visit Clark sent a handwritten note to Tom Brown, Grant Director, thanking the foundation for their time and consideration.

The Y was fortunate to receive a grant and Nanci drove by their office to pick up the check.

Tom told Nanci there was something he wanted to show her. He scurried down the hall and returned waving a paper in his hand, sharing the note saying that he was impressed with the CEO of the YMCA sending a handwritten note within 24 hours of the Y visit. Nanci said he showed it to her with such pride and admiration for Clark's gratitude. Although the note didn't necessarily secure the gift (the Y had an amazing relationship with the trustees), the gesture was the "icing on the cake that made the trustees feel their gift was appreciated and highly valued. Nancy said she would never forget that day.

Handwritten notes were one of Clark's personal ways to, as he coined it, "friend raise". If sincerely written, a handwritten communication has unimaginable power.

Clark first got inspired to "friend raise" by one board member—Bill Wilson. Bill is savvy, smooth, successful, and sincere. The two became fast friends when Clark became CEO in Nashville. Bill had a way of making people feel special just by being in his presence. He became a mentor and one of the key reasons Clark was so successful in Nashville.

Bill told Clark something one day that he never forgot, "Clark, the Y is very good at asking for money, but not so much about thanking people. I want us to be known for thanking people seven times for each gift."

Even today, 20 years after my husband first heard those words, neither Bill nor Clark have forgotten to thank folks. Recently Clark received a call from his friend who was in Naples, Florida, far away from the winter ice Nashville had just experienced. What was he doing? Bill was calling to say thanks for a donation we recently made to the Y. Each day he makes five phone calls to personally thank people who have given to the annual campaign. It's been over 15 years since Bill has been involved with the Y, but here he is back again, fully engaged, thanking folks. He "walks the walk", "talks the talk."

Clark took that early advice to heart and has written countless thank you notes to people....family, staff and volunteers. It has meant much as in today's world, handwritten notes are rare. So, when someone receives one in the mail, they rarely forget. I think it makes them more receptive to donate again and again.

Bill Wilson told me, *"I don't know any organization that worked as hard as we did at saying thank you."* He also recalls when *"we knew we were on to something."* It happened when *members of the Frist Foundation were invited to celebrate the opening of the new outdoor swimming pool of the East Y which at that time was located in the disadvantaged part of the city. The pool was the result of their generous gift. As the group arrived a thank you was on the marquee out front. Inside they were greeted by the preschool children smiling, clapping, and shaking hands with each member of the board. Even board chair, Margaret Maddox, who was in her 60s, agreed to don a swim suit and go down the slide! Within days after the celebration the foundation received a little thank you book that included photos of the special occasion. Pete Byrd of the Frist Foundation was overheard to comment that no one had every thanked them to this degree.*

Bill thought, "This is the largest foundation in town and no one's doing this? I think we ARE on to something."

One special thank you for Cal Turner, Dollar General CEO, was also notable for Bill. After Cal and his father pledged a major gift, Bill and Clark wanted to personally thank him. Julie Sistrunk (head of marketing and development) phoned Cal's secretary to plan a surprise thank you celebration. They brought balloons, thank you letters, signs AND a busload of pre-school children from the Y to the Dollar General headquarters unbeknownst to Cal. When he walked in there was music and cheering by the children. They all went up to the shocked donor and gave a thank you hug. Bill saw Cal's face---teary-eyed after being thanked in person by the very children most affected by him and his father's generosity.

From the time Bill ignited this idea to his last years as CEO in Houston, Clark has reminded his staff to say thank you. He says it best in the following email.

From: Clark Baker
Sent: Wednesday, March 26, 2014 9:15 AM
To: Everyone List
Subject: JUST SAY THANK YOU!!!!

We are closing in on the success of another year in our Annual Campaign. We plan to hit the $6.9mm annual goal, have already renewed our United Way $3mm allocation, so we seem to be on target to get close to $10mm!! This will be our largest amount raised ever....and we also know that many of you are working hard to bring in VICTORY. We have more center's showing 100% board giving and hitting or exceeding their goal than ever. THANKS to each of you, to your campaign leadership, and THANKS TO OUR DONORS AND BENEFACTORS.

I was once leading a capital campaign and the chair said..."there are many people out there saying PLEASE. I want us to be known as the campaign that said THANK YOU better than we said please." I learned a lot from that guy, and we came up with SAY THANK YOU SEVEN TIMES, in seven ways. A handshake, a personal phone call, a note, having a child write a card....you get it, SEVEN TIMES.

PLASTER THANK YOU SIGNS (tastefully, and w/out tacky tape). When we publically say THANK YOU it's not just for those who gave, BUT FOR THOSE WHO HAVE NOT YET GIVEN. It's an awareness that THERE IS SOMETHING GO-ING ON GOOD IN THIS Y, and our ability to serve people who are not able to pay.

SO, how are you going to say thank you? Will it be someone visiting the group exercise classes saying THANKS TO THOSE WHO GAVE so that kids can learn to swim, go to camp, play youth sports? Are you putting neat, bright, THANK YOU signage around your public areas of the facility? Are you putting

128

a THANK YOU on your marque? How creative can you be? Center Ex's and those responsible for the campaign own this, but bring your entire staff team in on the THANK YOU planning. Make it a big deal, celebrate the win!! THANKS TO YOU for your personal giving, your personal gift, for your United Way support, for being a faithful member of our staff.

JUST SAY THANKS.....it's not complicated, it's the right thing to do!! Make us proud. CLARK BAKER

In this time of high-tech, high-touch stands out. Handwritten notes are high-touch and worth every bit of time and effort...it's like gold.

CLARK BAKER

Clark treats the Vietnamese Dominican sisters to a ride on Rosie the firetruck at Camp Cullen, Houston.

GETTING THEM IN THE HUG
Deepen the Bench and Widen the Circle

It was 5:30 am in a Houston Starbucks that provides another illustration of how to connect with people. It was a chance encounter with former board member, Robert Duncan, chairman of Transwestern. He wrote the following:

"One morning years ago Clark asked me where I was going so early. I told him I was driving to Austin to see my mom. Showing his genuine concern in reliable fashion, he asked about her. I shared with him that she was suffering from Alzheimer's disease---and that things were getting worse by the day.

He immediately replied, 'What a beautiful time for the two of you to connect. You're such a wonderful son to be there for her. And she feels that, Robert. I will pray for her, as she grows closer to God, that she takes great joy in the magnificent legacy she has left with such a fine person as you.'

Those magnanimous words clutched my heart right then and have stayed with me ever since. Leadership is about giving of yourself and caring for others. Clark doesn't have to think a whole lot before talking...he just speaks from the heart. He characteristically humbles himself as God's servant. Clark genuinely cares for people and his feelings just flow. Clark is authentic. He is happy. His optimism is contagious. In his humble and unassuming fashion, his is ever so powerful. And he touches lives every day."

My husband gets people "in the hug" without much effort because he genuinely cares about people. Without even concentrating on it, he deepens the bench by getting to know people and usually doing something for them—it might be a kind word, an offer of prayers, sending flowers, a handwritten note, a quick "I'm thinking about you" email, a celebration of a person's birthday, or maybe reaching out financially and helping someone in a time of need.

Whatever the situation, Clark was able to widen the circle of friends and deepen relationships which directly affected the positive image of him and thus the YMCA.

I was always proud at how open and friendly so many people were to Clark when we attended national conventions. I quickly began to realize why—he had helped most everyone of those folks in some manner. It might have been a helpful reference for someone looking for a job, a charity that wanted his endorsement or financial support, or a personal note telling someone he understood they might be having a difficult time, etc. He was especially a cheerleader for the international group and they deeply were grateful.

I was always amazed at how he was charitable even to those who he knew had said things behind his back or were angry about a position he had taken. It's easy to be nice when others are kind to you, but the challenge is to be considerate and caring to those who are unkind and at times even mean. My partner could do that and do it with no hostility or resentment. I have always envied that kind of spirit. Living with someone like Clark has helped me become a more understanding person. Perhaps this is one of the traits of an outstanding leader---one of making no judgements and only remembering the good in people. Yes, Clark tried to get everyone he knew "in the hug"---strangers, staff, family, board members, and even those who were unpleasant.

Our oldest daughter, Christin, seemed to learn this lesson very well. In 2013 Christin was the specialist for the fine arts and humanics for the national headquarters--the YMCA of the USA (YUSA). She had that position for six years and was quite pleased that she had increased arts programs in many Ys across the country. Unfortunately, the movement went through a strategic plan and found it necessary to eliminate the art position. Of course Christin was devastated; but, like her father not only did she accept the decision with grace, she hosted her own goodbye karaoke party at a restaurant in the same building where YUSA is headquartered. It was a fabulous gathering where folks dropped by and sang and partied, wishing her well. She left YUSA with no resentment and with her head held high---something her father might have done in the same situation.

Another example of widening the circle with hospitality comes from YUSA Director of Health Partnerships and Policy, Katie Adamson:

"You can never be too welcoming or appreciative of guests at the Y. Clark Baker hosted the Centers for Disease Control and Prevention (CDC), key national health partners and the National Steps to a Healthier US community sites from across the country at his training site in Houston. There was no Houston community site in the group and there was no obvious 'return on investment' as Clark hosted the group for next to nothing. He rolled out the red carpet, had all staff on deck to serve. He utilized time on buses to visit the local Ys to have staff teach the visitors about the Ys Healthy Living work. He entertained with musical guests and offered great Y branded mugs and hats. All who attended felt as though they were 'home away from home'. That was our first Y event with the Centers for Disease Control and Prevention, and we are now in our 10th year of partnerships and the Y has secured tens of millions in funding from the federal agency in order to build healthier communities, individuals and families. Those guests, especially CDC, became part of the Y family on their visit to Houston and have been the best health partner to the Y nationally since we embarked on our healthy living innovation work."

When times were tough my spouse was at his best at widening the Y's circle of friends. An example was when Hurricanes Katrina and Rita hit New Orleans and the Gulf of Mexico in 2005. With Katrina, Houston housed thousands of refugees after the August storm. Through the generous support of successful business entrepreneur,

Jim McIngvale (Mattress Mack), Clark was able to open a makeshift YMCA at one of the refugee centers. I was amazed at what was done there! YMCA staff members Cindy Ferguson and Kelly Raglin helped to create and run the temporary center. Numerous basketball mini courts were set up where children could shoot hoops and play games. They assembled an enormous air conditioned tent in which children of all ages could read books, work puzzles, and play board games, etc. Even video games were set up for the teenagers. Countless Y staff from all over the city and the country came to help in any way they could. I enjoyed volunteering a number of days, and it was amazing how kind and understanding everyone was to the families of those who no longer had a home. You could tell by their faces how lost the parents felt, but how they were grateful for a place where their children could run and play safely.

When Hurricane Rita hit just one month after Katrina in 2005, it affected Houston with not only high winds but a tremendous amount of rain. Many residents lost electricity and had no water. Again, the Y offered free showers and phone charging at their facilities. Phone charging was especially welcomed.

It was on a particular sweltering day that Clark happened to receive a call from someone offering two truckloads of ICE! That was such a blessing as the heat was unbearable without air conditioning. My husband offered a portion of the ice to some of the centers who were in need; and then he realized that the Dominican Vietnamese Sisters had no AC at their convent. Clark rode with the truck and

134

helped unload ice. The sisters felt compassion for the apartment complex nearby, so they decided to share with those folks. The gift had a nice ripple effect.

It must be noted that numerous YMCAs called from across the nation to offer support after both hurricanes. Clark was grateful, and he was able to help more people than he ever thought possible through their generous donations.

How is your organization deepening the bench, widening the circle? Get out in your community and share your talents. You and your business will reap respect and rewards that never seemed possible.

Clark and I getting the Vietnamese sisters "in the hug".

Spread love everywhere you go. Let no one ever come to you without leaving happier.
MOTHER TERESA

Clark in front of the mantel at the Clark D. Baker Lodge, Joe C. Davis Center.

MAYOR OF STARBUCKS
Work, Play, Pray HARD

At first glance the coffee shop on the corner of Augusta and Woodway in Houston seems like "just another Starbucks." But that's where the comparison stops. This establishment has become a hodgepodge of fun-loving, light-hearted teasing, eclectic folks who care deeply for others and show it. This is the same Starbucks where Clark met Robert Duncan. In fact, the front page in the Houston Chronicle featured this unique group in an article on December 22, 2014.

Each morning the group meets in the corner of Starbucks. There is no time set and no one knows who might show up, but you can bet there will be some portion of the group or all of them especially on celebratory events like birthdays. They banter back and forth, laughing and joking. They truly boost the spirit of the entire restaurant. The employees love their presence as they are so friendly and giving.

Each Christmas, the dean of the group, John Egan (former NBA basketball star and coach of the Houston Rockets from the 1970s), collects money for the employees. Most Christmas gifts end up being around $1000 for each barista. It doesn't stop there. If John hears of someone in need, he goes to his Starbucks' friends and everyone contributes to the cause.

Clark was part of the group while we lived in Houston. It was not uncommon for him to buy drinks for people standing in line or for the group to pitch in and buy new tires for an employee who was down on his luck. Jeanne Ng, the manager, joined in the fun and allowed cakes and dessert to be brought in for various celebrations.

Clark loved this group and in Houston, his breakfast at Starbucks became part of his morning routine. I believe that beginning his day with such a lively group helped him tackle any problems he would encounter. Because of Clark's daily presence and his congenial attitude he was sometimes known as the Mayor of Starbucks.

One day he came home and said, "Carolyn, I want to have a 25th birthday party for one of our baristas. He's never had a birthday party…ever.

"Honey, I don't even know this guy, but what the heck. Let's do it."

We had the event catered using a local popular restaurant, hired a pianist, and crammed the entire group into our loft to celebrate a 25th birthday for a very grateful young man.

I especially loved the diversity at the gathering….from CEOs, teachers, business managers, retired executives to the baristas and their spouses or significant others. There were those who wore beautifully tailored suits or casual khakis and vests to multi-tattooed baristas with long hair and piercings all over their bodies. The group genuinely enjoyed each other and the barista experienced a birthday he'll never forget.

Clark's time in Houston was enriched by this group whose members also gathered at the lovely home of one of the most faithful of the group, David Skarke. These two buddies used to love to banter back and forth about Catholics and Episcopalians. I was fortunate to get to know David as a number of times David, Clark, and I would share an evening meal together. He even surprised us by hosting a goodbye brunch in honor of Clark's retirement, which included all members of our family who had come to celebrate the special occasion, plus all the Starbucks gang. It meant the world to us.

Since his departure, my husband has continued to stay in touch with members of the group via email and never misses a chance to drop in when he visits Houston.

Frequent patron of Starbucks, Tim Goodwin, penned this:

"I know Clark through mornings at Starbucks. I have always been impressed at how he always has a group around him engaging in conversation. When he is not there, the group is unorganized. That is why he is known as the Mayor of Starbucks at Woodway and Augusta. He is a great guy and always brightens up the morning for my wife and me!"

Besides his Starbucks "play yard," Clark enjoys being with his family. He especially loves to watch the antics of his grandchildren. Visiting with them is considered a treat because they live in another city.

One of his other times of play is boating. I've known very few times when we have been without some sort of cruiser. Our children grew up spending weekends boating on various lakes where we have lived.

Clark recalls one time just after he sold one of our boats, daughter Christin seemed very sad for a week. A friend asked why the gloomy face.

Granddaughter, Annabelle, pretends to drive.

She replied, "We're boatless!"

One of our favorite boats while in Florida. The girls especially loved to jump from the boat and float around in a cove. Water skiing and playing on a seadoo were added as they grew up. Going to the lake was such a great way to be with family and friends—we have loved every moment.

Clark also loves classic cars. He drives me crazy with the "Velocity channel" with the

incessant chant of the auctioneer bid calling. But he just loves seeing how folks have refurbished those beautiful old machines. He knows hometown friends and notable citizens by the cars they drive. Even today if you refer to specific board members, he can tell you the year and model of the automobile each drove.

I'm happy to say that I believe when he's not working, Clark enjoys spending time with me. We delight in traveling, going to movies, dining out, and simply being together. We don't have to say anything---there's something about the mere presence of each other that is soothing. I recall one time I remained in Nashville some 12 months after he had moved, waiting for our home to sell. We tried to see each other as much as possible, but it was costly and I was still working.

One day he phoned, "Carolyn, I think it's time for you to move here no matter what."

He laughingly added, "Some people don't think you exist, that I am 'making up' that I have a wife."

I got it. Within a month, I was in Houston.

Carved into the mantel of the Clark D. Baker Lodge at YMCA Camp Widjiwagen in Nashville is Clark's coined phrase, "Work Hard, Play Hard, Pray Hard." I feel the "work hard" part of the trio has been out of balance much of his Y tenure---spending a great deal of time trying his best to make whatever Y he has led to be successful. That said, he has NEVER neglected his prayer life, starting from his early experiences in Catholic school and spending time with his favorite aunt, Sister Frances Joan. And he treasured his times with family, especially as our daughters were growing up. The girls always felt secure and loved by their father.

Below is what our youngest daughter, Caroline, wrote about her father:

"In the side pocket of my purse are a variety of items that I keep so that they are not accessible to others. I don't need them daily, but they are there when I do need them. Inside that pocket is a card that has resided in every stylish purse I have owned since 1997. On one side is a note from my father that says, "To Caroline—one of the finest God made—on her Search Weekend—from one who loves her dearly. Dad, 20 March 1997." On the other side is a quote from Thomas Merton. It reads:

> *My Lord God, I have no idea where I am going. I do not see the road ahead of me. I cannot know for certain where it will end. Nor do I really know myself, and the fact that I think that I am following your will does not mean that I am actually doing so. But I believe that the desire to please you does in fact please you. And I hope that I have that desire in all that I am doing. I hope that I will never do anything apart from that desire. And I know that if I do this you will lead me by the right road though I may know nothing about it. Therefore I will trust you always though I may seem to be lost and in the shadow of death. I will not fear, for you are ever with me, and you will never leave me to face my perils alone.*

Every once in a while, while grabbing an insurance or gift card, I will pick up that letter from my father and read it. I often think about his path in leadership and how he always stayed so positive and lifted people up at all times. He had a vision, but when I think of Thomas Merton's prayer, I wonder how many times Dad didn't know what would lie ahead, but he trusted his faith and trusted the path on which God sent him. His faith is unshakable, and I have never seen him in doubt. Growing up in our house, the 'it will work out' or 'have faith, give it to God' mentality was reinforced constantly. Maybe Dad did feel scared inside or feared what may happen during different times; however, he seemed to continue gliding along, facing challenges without fear. Looking back, he used his faith in God to guide him, even when he wasn't sure where exactly he was going.

A few years ago I participated in a year-long Leadership Development cohort with my job. We discussed leadership versus management, with the overarching theme being that leaders rise above managers in the long run. My favorite quote is from Kouzes and Posner that states, 'Leadership is the art of mobilizing others to want to struggle for shared aspirations.' I honestly can't think of a better example of visionary leadership then my father as it relates to this definition of leadership. Dad can mobilize people. He can make people want to move for the work that benefits all. Some even say they were working so hard and didn't realize it, but it was all inspired by Clark David Baker.

Let me tie these ideas together. My dad exemplifies visionary leadership. He is the master of this work, and the YMCA benefitted from his vision and style. But our family got the best gift of all. We got to have a visionary father. A father who wrote us notes, sent us little cards with inspiration, came to our events, 'showed up' as he would say. He didn't talk about it or explain what he was doing, but he just lived that way, day after day. His energy was and still is contagious. I love talking with him about life, about work, about family, about anything. There are times that come our way, where I don't know where I am going or if the path I am on or decisions I have made are the right ones. However, seeing the example of Dad's faith and steadfast commitment to whatever he was doing, even if he wasn't sure he was doing the right thing, helps me through those times. I haven't ever told him that. Maybe I should. But either way, I'll keep reaching in my purse pocket to find inspiration in my dad's little card he gave me. He probably doesn't even remember giving it to me, as he gave us so many, but a little tap on the side of my purse reminds me that this is life--life will go on, just keep moving, and have faith in God who will never leave us alone."

Clark did his best to balance his family life and career. I'm proud of his efforts.

Even today, when Clark is asked to speak to young staff at various YMCAs, he reminds them to balance working hard, playing hard, praying hard.

Clark with daughters Christin and Caroline.

 Far and away the best prize that life offers is the chance to work hard at work worth doing.
THEODORE ROOSEVELT

Clark's portrait when he first moved to Chattanooga, TN.

SUZANNE'S STORY
Be a Professional Role Model

When I asked for stories about Clark and his leadership, Suzanne Goswick's touched me deeply. Suzanne is currently the vice president of human resources and leadership development at the YMCA of Metropolitan Dallas in Texas. Her story alone is worthy of a chapter by itself. It is the perfect way to share a lesson about being a role model.

"My story of Clark Baker is not only of extraordinary leadership, but also of blind trust and spontaneous compassion. A story not uncommon to those whose lives and careers were touched by Clark. A gesture that has had a lasting and profound affect upon my life; it has impacted the way I build relationships, my philosophy on leadership, and my steadfast belief in the mission of the YMCA.

In 1999, with my career well underway at the Dallas YMCA, my most promising opportunity seemed to exist in Tennessee. A recent divorcee as well as graduate, I was ready for the next step in my life and in my career. Clark hired me and I prepared myself and my three children for the relocation to Nashville. It was a new life, a new career, and a new beginning. After a great deal of consideration, it was decided my eldest son would remain in Dallas to complete his senior year. I knew no one, had no relationships, no support, and had left one son behind. I was elated at the opportunity, yet anxious of the unknown.

I was only two weeks on the job when I got the call...the call that every parent dreads, the call that your child is missing. When my son was found several hours later, he was disoriented; unaware of who and where he was. He was taken to the hospital and immediately admitted to the psychiatric ward for evaluation. He was in crisis, becoming increasingly delusional and violent by the hour. I agonized over my choices throughout the night; in dilemma of how to help my son and not destroy my new career

145

and our future. With the assurance that my family would attend to his care, I remained in Nashville. The stress was extremely overwhelming, and yearning for support, I confided in a co-worker. Resolute to separate my personal life from my career, I went through the motions; attending meetings, meeting members of the community, and connecting with peers. When I returned to the office that day there was a note on my desk, a note from Clark. A note to me from a man who barely knew me; I hadn't earned his trust and I hadn't proven myself. And yet, there it was; a plane ticket to return home, arrangements for the care of my other two children, and the note that simply said; 'take all the time you need and return when you can.'

Extraordinary leadership, blind trust, and spontaneous compassion were not only displayed that day, but in almost every facet of Clark Baker's unassuming guidance. He did for me what should have been done, with no thought of self-gratification. By demonstrating empathy, he taught me to be empathic. Throughout my time with him, he continually demonstrated what it is to be a true servant leader. His actions inspired me to reach my full potential. He changed the way I thought about leadership and influenced how I manage today. He taught me that true results happen through relationships and that leadership should be used as a means to obtain the general good, not as a desired personal end. That trust should be freely given and integrity means living in alignment with the ideals we embrace.

I often reflect on his example as I build my own team and relationships with peers, colleagues and family. I take the time to listen and to put myself in another's shoes. I strive to treat someone as I would want to be treated. Through the examples of Clark Baker and the organizational leadership philosophy of the YMCA, I believe that servant leadership opens doors. It allows opportunities and potential to be realized and enables one to develop their dreams. I believe our actions can lead to infinite, profound inspiration, and because of his actions, I am a better person, a better leader, and forever grateful."

The website "Roots of Action" (rootsofaction.com) is a research-based resource for parents, schools, and communities. The site reveals results of a research study on the top five qualities of a role model by Dr. Marilyn Price-Mitchell. The study focused on young people, but adults had similar answers when they reflected on role models in their lives. How many of the following do you find in yourself? I believe Clark embodies all five qualities that Dr. Price-Mitchell listed:

*Passion and Ability to Inspire—Clark's passion for his life-long work was motivational and he inspired others throughout his career.

*Clear Set of Values---my husband's values rarely deviated from his daily living. Sometimes I slip and use a curse word, not Clark. We've been together for over 40 years and I've rarely, if ever, heard him say anything inappropriate. He "talks the talk" and "walks the walk."

*Commitment of Community---Clark excels in this quality. Even today, being retired, he continues to give

Mark and Clark at the beach.

of himself….serving on eight boards and volunteering when he is asked.

*Selflessness and Acceptance of Others--- This to me is such a gift---especially in our country which, at this time, is so polarized. Clark seems to find the good in all with whom he meets…regardless of religious or political affiliation. When it came to those with special needs, he again is benevolent and was especially kind to my brother, Mark, who had Down syndrome. When I wanted to bring him to our home or on vacation with us, my husband didn't think twice, he immediately agreed and helped to make his stay a pleasant experience. When many people disregard the elderly, Clark is drawn to them. I am envious of this characteristic---I'd like to think I'm accepting of others, but my husband far outshines me in this area.

*Ability to Overcome Obstacles--- My partner has overcome a number of obstacles in his life beginning with his childhood. I had to have a few breast biopsies and surgery to remove half my thyroid (all were benign results). During this time Clark was there for me (it was difficult as he finds hospital visits challenging) every step of the way. He was my rock. While holding me and drying my tears, he always found something positive and made me feel so secure and hopeful. He has never lost his upbeat attitude even during difficult opportunities in his career. Dr. Price-Mitchell cited this quote by Booker T. Washington in her article: "Success is to be measured not so much by the position that one has reached in life as by the obstacles which one has overcome." Clark has triumphed over hurdles and continues to look to the future in a positive light.

When chatting with my husband about the responsibility a leader has in being a role model, he recalled times he has given insight to a situation or had the opportunity to have an impact in personal situations. It's in these times one is given the possibility to perform random of acts of kindness. Clark has purchased blazers and clothing for some staff members who didn't have the extra funds or even the time to shop. Visiting folks in the hospital, attending funerals, celebrating special birthdays, dropping by flowers to personnel who were sick at home, greeting and getting to know everyone involved with your organization are all ways he believes helped be a positive role model. People are watching and in today's world, people are recording your actions. Don't think for a minute that your actions go unnoticed. A priest once looked my husband in the eye and said, "Clark, in your position, you can be a role model by the way you handle situations. People will follow your lead."

 If you are what you should be you will set the world on fire.
ST. CATHERINE OF SIENA

Photo from a Continental Magazine article "The Y Guy", September 2004.

REFLECTIONS OF A JOURNEY
Visionaries Learn from Every Place They Serve

Clark's love for the YMCA was so strong that he had visions of its greatness since walking through the doors as a child on scholarship. He read the history of the Y and committed it to memory. Frequently he cited passages from the 1881 Young Men's Christian Association Handbook. Reading a passage to me he commented, "Isn't it amazing

Clark referred to this 1888 hand-book during his entire career.

how so much of this is still relevant today?" As a final going away gift to the Houston staff, Clark presented each member with a copy of his treasured Y "Bible."

Clark's vision for each YMCA with which he was associated was tied to the needs of the community, always wanting to leave it in better shape than when he arrived. His vision included making the Y one of the most respected institutions in its respective community---one which everyone would hold in high esteem and one that was innovative, yet responsive to the needs of all, rich and poor. He loved that this organization was a place of common ground...where a millionaire might be working out next to truck driver. All are welcome at the YMCA. Clark was always so proud to say, "The Y is one place where we take you from womb to tomb. We have prenatal classes, tiny tot swim, teen programs, adult exercise classes, and classes for seniors."

My husband clearly understood each community where we resided. From his hometown in Washington, Indiana, to his last assignment in Houston, Texas, he did his homework, observing and learning what worked in the past and what might be needed for the future. Each move brought different challenges. He would patiently watch and listen, recognizing the current situation of each Y. After careful study, he could then share his vision. This process worked well as he had staff and board all supporting him. It actually become THEIR vision.

Clark learned from every place he's been. He took what he learned to every new assignment, adapting his standards of excellence and his commitment to mission to each location.

In his hometown of Washington, he visualized a fantastic indoor swimming pool where all ages in the community could come and swim during those cold Indiana winters. At that time the only available place to swim was the outdoor city pool which only opened in the summer. Through his first capital campaign, that pool became a reality. He gleaned much through that process---the strategy of how to run a successful campaign began in that small town of 12,000.

He learned organizational skills and structures while working in Orlando. CEO Bill Phillips could organize his way out of anything and Clark gained knowledge while observing and studying Bill's competence in this area. Clark told me, "We were just coming out of a severe recession and Florida was particularly hit hard. The first line of business was stabilizing the operation. Bill and his board began to look at expansion as communities were asking for their services. We acquired land and built the West Orange County Y. We then proceeded to add two more Ys in Deland and the Golden Triangle. That was extraordinary to have three Ys come to fruition after a deep recession."

One story from his Orlando experience helped remind my spouse that he needed to also learn from his staff.

Being an excellent connector, Clark had been wanting to meet the owner of a national dog food company who resided in the city. He had tried several times to call his office in order to meet the gentleman. It seems he was always "out" or "unavailable." Clark went a different route, asking a number of business leaders who worked out at the Y if anyone knew him well or could possibly help him with being able to meet the entrepreneur—no luck. For the time being, Clark dropped the idea to pursue getting to know "Mr. Dog Food."

One bright early morning while driving into the Y parking lot, Clark was jarred by a discordant sound coming from his back bumper. A gigantic black Cadillac had just rammed into his car! An elderly gentleman shuffled toward him saying, "I'm so sorry about this, I just didn't see you while I was backing. I'm at fault here and will be happy to take care of the damage. My name is Gaines, Clarence Gaines."

Clark was shocked to realize that this was the very man who he had tried to reach innumerable times. Grasping his hand in a mighty handshake he said, "Why, Mr. Gaines, I've been wanting to meet you for a long time. What brings you here to the Y?" Clark asked, forgetting all about his damaged car.

"Well, son, I come to the YMCA three mornings a week for a massage. I just love your masseur, Austin Allen. Austin is blind, but he's very good. I rarely miss an appointment."

All this time and effort to find a way to meet Mr. Gaines, when all he had to do was ask some his staff members. They are the folks who really know the members. Just like the old saying, "only your hairdresser knows," Clark realized that sometimes, "Only your massage therapist knows!"

In Chattanooga Clark discovered how to work with old wealth. Chattanooga is an exceptionally beautiful city nestled next to the Tennessee River and the stunning Lookout, Elder, and Signal mountains. We lived on Signal Mountain where I still have fond memories of driving up and down winding roads and hairpin curves. Even today when I close my eyes I can smell the fresh air as we drove up the mountain with windows down. It was wonderful experience for our family.

Neither Clark nor I knew much about Chattanooga before his arrival in 1982 as CEO of the YMCA. There was only the song, Chattanooga Choo Choo, which he had occasionally hummed and played on the organ. It didn't take him long to meet and get to know many of the city leaders. They all seemed eager to see the Y succeed and wanted to support their new young CEO. Many of the folks came from old wealth. They were exceedingly proud of Chattanooga and had long pedigrees. Clark wanted to learn and get to know them all. In the late 1970's this was relatively a small city, perfect in terms of size for the young executive to wrap his arms around.

Clark still treasures memories of Chattanooga and the community where the old wealth gave so much. He was able with their help to renovate numerous centers and add a new Y in nearby Rosswell, Georgia.

Clark also tried an innovative program---an adult day-care center. I remember visiting the center and noticing how beautifully it had been decorated, making it seem like home for those elderly who were served while their caregivers got desperately needed breaks. Clark was way ahead of his time with this idea, however; within a year it had to be closed due to lack of funding. Now, adult day care centers are found all over the United States. Another innovation was a pre-school center housed in and run by the Y---at that time, too, this was a rare occurrence. That pre-school is still in existence today.

Because of the connections and make-up of the board, representing old Chattanooga and old money, Clark was able to raise several million dollars in less than five months for much needed renovations. It was because of those relationships that we had one of the most influential boards in the city, and perhaps in the country. Some members, like Nelson Irvine and Bill Pettway, were fourth generation board members.

In Nashville Clark put everything he had previously learned into practice.

It all came together when we arrived in 1987 in the midst of another recession. His board was dynamic and not afraid to boldly campaign for a growing Y. He was able to build eight new YMCAs and a camp due to the untiring spirit and giving of his board, staff, and the community. This Y raised over $50 million dollars for needed projects. Back then a facility could be built for $3 or $4 million dollars, so this was a monumental sum at that time.

Ridley Wills, an historian and community leader who chaired the search committee that hired Clark, wrote, *"Clark is the best and most effective YMCA CEO that I have ever known. He absolutely put Nashville on the top of the YMCA chart. When Clark ambled over here from Chattanooga, we were about the 35th largest YMCA in the country. When the Bakers moved to Houston, we were number SEVEN---Phenomenal."*

Finally, the Houston YMCA became Clark's great laboratory. This giant city had the most opportunities than any city in the nation---success, diversity, and ALL of it was BIG. They aren't kidding when people say everything in Texas is done in a big way. Again he was blessed with a board that had his same shared vision. Just as with Nashville, the Houston Y board was visionary, enthusiastic, and determined to grow the Y to meet the needs of this massive metropolis. During his tenure, he was able to construct 12 new facilities and totally rebuild Camp Cullen.

My husband wanted to encourage his entire staff to join him and the board in their vision of progress. David Snow, Development Director for the Houston YMCA, sent me a quote he found that Clark wrote shortly after he arrived to become CEO:

"Each of us is merely a small instrument, all of us after accomplishing our mission will disappear, only that which we have left behind will endure, it is that for which we are called… it is for that purpose that we organize to carry out this work, in this place, at this time. I invite you to join me in this journey, to be the best we can, each and every day….. Come with me." Baker 2002

Community garden at the Trotter Y in Houston. Board member and philanthropist, Howard Tellepsen built June's cottage (in honor of his mother) which overlooks the garden.

Clark was a great delegator---he hired dynamic staff so that he could focus on forward-thinking long-range needs. His vision brought a chaplain to the Y, backpacks to children in need, community gardens at a number of YMCAs, apartment outreach centers, water-wise outreach programs which helped children with water safety skills, Springfield College satellite campus helping those interested to work toward bachelor's and master's degrees, and numerous other programs that helped the expansive Houston community. If you had an idea, Clark encouraged you to give it a try.

The Houston budget grew from $67 million to $125 million and fundraising more than doubled. Clark's team raised over $200 million in private gift support. All those skills gained from Washington, Orlando, Chattanooga, and Nashville helped with his success in Houston.

As Clark shared, "I've never been wiser."

Good leaders create a vision, passionately articulate the vision, and relentlessly drive the vision to completion.

JACK WELCH

Carolyn and Clark at the groundbreaking for the Carolyn and Clark Baker Science and Arts Center.

Clark with VP of Programs, Shawn Borzelleri, at the dedication of the YMCA Miracle League's adaptive fields in Houston.

EPILOGUE
LEAVE WHILE THE BAND IS STILL PLAYING
Retiring With Grace

The occurrence comes for most everyone---a difficult decision, for sure! How does a person determine when to retire? Advice was given by many---Clark's older brother, Dick, recommended he not retire too early. Many other friends gave similar advice.

He had a date in mind, but several board members cornered him and convinced their CEO to stay one extra year. Then again when that year ended another opportunity came to ask Clark to stay. I remember it well.

Three incredible longtime powerful board members Dick Weekly, Scotty Arnoldy, and John Duncan invited Clark and me to come to California to spend the weekend

with them and their wives. The seaside home of David Weekly is one of the most beautiful I have ever had the pleasure of visiting. Nestled on the coast of the Pacific, the views are breathtaking. One can sit outside having a glass of wine while watching the sunset, as

Weekley's, Duncan's, Baker's and John Arnoldy enjoy the beauty of California.

waves crash against the craggy giant rocks. We enjoyed the company of these stellar individuals each of whom has had incredible life experiences. John Duncan, my favorite Texan storyteller, was in his best storytelling mood and I simply wanted be like a sponge...soaking in his glorious stories told in his special charming way only John can do…

At one point during the weekend, the tone changed, and the conversation took on a more serious mood. I believe John brought up the topic. Here is how I recall the discussion. One of three spoke up, "Clark, you know we all feel you have been an outstanding leader of the Houston YMCA, and we know you are planning to retire soon, but we'd like you to consider staying a little longer."

My husband paused a moment. He then thanked the men for their strong support and told them he felt very complimented by their sincere desire to have him stay. He finished by saying this, "You know, I feel one should leave while the band is still playing. I've had such a great ride here and I want to leave at the top of my game. Thank you, but I feel it's a good time for me to retire. I wanted to complete two capital campaigns: the campaign for new adaptive fields and sports complex for the Miracle League and the campaign to rebuild Camp Cullen. By the time I leave those should be almost complete. It's time to go home, gentlemen."

The guys told Clark they understood, but had to ask. It was a perfect compliment for my husband and so special that they held him in such high regard. For 50 years Clark had been involved with the Y. It was only natural that retiring would not be an easy decision. After all, this was an organization that had been such a big part of his life.

Clark retired on February 6, 2015. Not wanting a big expensive event just for him, he accepted the suggestion to celebrate his retirement along with other volunteers at the annual Y dinner. This would not be as costly or time consuming as two separate events. It was such a lovely event and Clark felt so affirmed. Professional event planner, Board member, and friend, Gerri Ayers, took special effort to help make the gathering one Clark would forever remember. The entire Y staff simply made every effort to make the evening memorable for all of us----we had close family members and friends fly in from all over the country. It was, indeed, a night that Clark and I will fondly have etched in our minds forever. It ended with the announcement that the new arts and science center at camp would be named after Clark and after me! I was deeply touched by their thoughtfulness to include my name.

It's been over a year since Clark and I left Houston. Moving back to Nashville was a good decision. Our eldest daughter recently moved back and we now live closer to our youngest daughter and her family. We had wisely purchased a home in our old neighborhood during the recession when housing prices were falling. Other than trying to scale down furnishings into one house, the move was seamless.

It took Clark a little while to adjust to retirement. For one thing, he has had an assistant for almost as many years as we've been married---and that's 42 years! He was used to these wonderful ladies (yes, they've all been women) checking his schedule, making arrangements, and making sure he knew where he was supposed to be. I told his assistant in Houston, Mary Norton, that I missed her as much as Clark, as he has already mixed up a number of appointments. I admire her even more, now realizing how integral she was to his daily schedule.

I have been teasing my husband that he is retired in name only. He currently is the chair of the St. Thomas Hospital/Health Board and is a member of at least seven other boards. He also is enjoying working part time for the Nashville YMCA in development. He was hired by two people HE once hired himself, Dan Dummermuth (CEO of the Middle Tennessee YMCA) and Julie Sistrunk (Development Director). When I chided him for doing too much he responded, "One day the phone won't ring asking me to be as involved. So right now, while I'm willing and able, I will be of service when asked."

I wondered if Clark ever worries that he will soon be

forgotten. I recently received this text from Christin, our oldest daughter, which makes me think he shouldn't be too concerned:

"I'm on the phone with Constance Miller (friend of Christin who works for Daxko, Inc.—Software Provider for YMCAs and other nonprofits) and there were Y people at Daxko and Baker's name came up and someone had never met dad and asked what it was like to meet Clark Baker and Constance said, 'It's like the Y at its best, giving you a big hug and great advice'."

He is happy and still making a difference....just on a lesser level, but significant all the same.

The band continues to play for Clark...

Clark with his namesake, Deacon CLARK Tuss, born June 2, 2016

Clark and Carolyn with their grandchildren---June Frances, Deacon Clark, and Annabelle Ruth.

ACKNOWLEDGEMENTS

> " Let gratitude be the pillow
> upon which you kneel to say
> your nightly prayer
>
> ## MAYA ANGELOU "

Clark strongly believes in saying thank you. Going along with that theme, I would like to say thanks for all the people and their kindnesses bestowed upon me as I journeyed to write this book.

Thank you to all those who took time to respond for my request for stories about Clark and leadership. It is because of YOU this book has been enriched far more than if it had been written solely from my perspective.

Over forty-five years ago, my sister, Dianna Lavoie, encouraged my relationship with Clark from that very first date in Heidelberg, Germany. Thanks, dear sister, as you were right about what a great guy he was and continues to be. "I want him for my brother-in-law" was a pretty darn strong endorsement.

My mother, Ruth Simpson (and my father) also liked Clark and brags about him at every opportunity. I admire Mom for her strength and courage which I continually strive to emulate. My mother loved my first book. She even kept extras in her car in case she ran into someone who might want to purchase it. Our daily talks inspired me to keep working on my second book in spite of constant interruptions.

My nephew and Godchild, Jean-Paul Lavoie, was the first to respond when I asked for suggestions for titles for the book. I ended up taking his suggestion.

My editor suggested I add a time line. The first person I thought of to help with this task was Nick Simpson. My nephew is a talented artist and kindly agreed to draw a clever time line of Clark's career.

Julie Sistrunk and Lori Swan were not only incredible staff who helped Clark with his success in Nashville, but I credit them for caring so much for my husband during challenging times. I will forever be grateful for their love and support.

John Duncan is my favorite storyteller. He has heart the size of Texas (his home state). John was supportive of my first book, "Last to Leave Home" where he has a quote on the book jacket. He was kind enough to do so in this current endeavor.

Cindy Ferguson has been a life-long friend. She worked for Clark beginning in Orlando and followed him to Chattanooga and on to Houston. She truly helped with our girls when they were young. She continues to support both Clark and me.

Michelle Barber and Marjorie Snow are two of my dearest friends who have supported me in all my projects. Both encouraged me when I penned my first book. Michelle even had a book signing at St. Matthew Catholic Church when she was involved with the women's club.

When I requested input from Clark's list of friends and family, Mary Norton (Clark's assistant) was kind enough to send out the list and forward me any stories which came to her. Clark has always been close to Mary (I'm a big fan too).

Elizabeth Harper-Neeld taught a class in Houston titled "Writing the Nonfiction Book". Because of that class and the confidence she instilled, I was able to publish two books. Elizabeth continues to inspire me and was kind enough to coach me as I began book two.

My daughters Christin Baker and Caroline Baker Tuss are so special and have been encouraging each time I've written. Christin has listened to my ideas and was gracious enough to make suggestions in addition to contributing three stories which had added much to the book.

Grand-daughters Annabelle and June Frances are simply a joy to be with—being with them refreshes my soul. After I return from visits, I can sit down at my desk and compose as their youth and spirit stimulate my creative juices. Now I have a new grandson to inspire me. Deacon Clark Tuss was born June 2, 2016.

Kendal Gladdish edited my first book and kindly agreed to edit this manuscript. She is excellent and insists on donating her fee to Camp Cullen and Camp Widjiwagan.

David Read worked on my first book cover and has been kind enough to do so again. David is so creative and I am ever so grateful for his quality work.

Kim Lagunas from the Houston Y was such a support in researching and emailing numerous photos to be used in the book. I am very grateful for your efforts.

It's important to be able to trust your publisher. Paula Shelton at Josten's is not only exceedingly competent, but she gives great advice. She helped to guide me on both book projects.

Layne Moore prepared the layout for my first book and I was thrilled when he accepted my request to work on my second project. He is so kind and works diligently until I'm happy with the outcome of the layout.

When I spoke with Clark about possible folks to write the forward to this book, we both agreed that we needed to ask Jerry Panas. Jerry has a very successful fundraising company and has written numerous books. He and Clark have been friends since they met over thirty years ago. We were so pleased that Jerry agreed to write the forward to the book.

Dare I forget to mention my husband, Clark. Thank you, my love, my best friend, for sharing your life with me. Just watching the way you have led, the way you love people from all walks of life, and the way you give of yourself is astonishing. Your sensitivity and caring of those you mentored, of those you employed, and of those you befriended makes you remarkable in so many ways. I realize that I have been truly blessed to be by your side for over 44 years.

If there is anyone I've left out, I apologize profusely. I simply know that my intention is to share ideas for leadership which I have witnessed in my husband's successful career, therefore helping anyone wishing to become a visionary leader.

So I thank anyone and everyone who has somehow contributed to this venture.

Each time I kneel I thank my God for all who have crossed my path and given me inspiration to write-- My God bless you all.

ACKNOWLEDGEMENTS

Clark's Gratitude List

Clark asked me if he personally could acknowledge people in his life who helped him in his journey to become a visionary leader. I whole-heartedly consented. My husband is deeply grateful to those special individuals mentioned in the book. In addition he wanted to mention the following folks who helped him in his career and with life's lessons.

Washington, Indiana (Clark's hometown)

--William E. Summers, Jr. (Bill) was on Clark's first capital campaign committee and was the main driver behind the Gwaltney Aquatic Center in Washington, Indiana...Clark's very first successful campaign.

--Monsieur William Lautner was Clark's pastor and teacher from the time he was in 3rd grade. He was a great leader and Clark became close to him when he was given opportunities to serve in the church. Father invited him to become a reader and song leader at Mass, plus an invitation to play the organ.

--Clark thanks his first fundraising consultant, Bill Kemp. Bill taught Clark his first lessons in financial development and was the key reason he was successful in the Washington, Indiana, campaign.

--Ken Parsons has been Clark's friend since the 1970s when they commuted to Indiana University together. He performed the first physical audit of the Washington Y, doing so pro bono. Personal note: When Clark and I married, Jodi and Ken became close friends and spent many happy times together in Washington.-

-Clark's friend since the 1960s was Charlie O'Dell. Charlie and Clark became fast friends, with boating being a favorite pastime. Personal note: I came to view them as the little town's Tom Sawyer and Huck Finn. As soon as they found a moment free they'd grab their towels, hook up the boat, and head for the "boat club"They solved life's problems while passing time at the boat club.

--Clark's oldest friend was Richard Smith. They met when Clark got his tricycle stuck and Richie's dad came to rescue him. Richie's parents, Oliva and Eugene, welcomed him into their family and he was in a sense their adopted son. Eugene hired Clark...it was his first job at the Y. Later Richie had a career in the army----retiring as a Lt. Colonel.

--David Snow, Clark's closet friend, began their relationship in Indiana....they were rivals in elementary school and friends in high school at Washington Catholic. They've been colleagues in many successful endeavors over the years.

--Sister Michaela, SP, had a lasting effect on him as she was his homeroom teacher throughout high school. Everytime he visited his aunt at St. Mary of the Woods, Clark would also look up Sister Micahaela and visit with her.

--Clark's aunt, Sr. Frances Joan Baker, SP, was such a close relative that they used to have breakfast together between masses on Sunday. It was fun being with her as she had such a joyful spirit and was one of the most beautiful human beings Clark and I ever met.

 --Frances introduced Clark to Sister Joan who was a fantastic organist. Clark and I both enjoyed watching her "tickle the ivories" as she had such passion when she played. She inspired Clark's passion for playing the organ.

 --Clark was named after his Uncle Albert Clark. He and Aunt Fanny played an integral part of Clark's early life. They took him to plays, carnivals, county fairs, and bought him his first moped scooter. Clark spent countless hours at their small farm where one of his favorite pastimes was riding Francis the mule.

--Nell Keller, the church organist, gave Clark (before choir practice on Wednesdays) a key to the organ so he could open it up and play while she slowly maneuvered up the steep winding stairs. She was old and it took a good deal of time to make it up to the choir loft where she had to take time to catch her breath. Clark didn't mind as it gave him time to play. My husband can't read a note of music, but plays by ear with such passion you would swear he was a concert pianist. Nell taught Clark about the keys and the stops on the organ. She didn't realize the gift she gave him as he later played the organ at mass for years at St. Simon in Washington, at St. Thomas Chapel and Holy Family church in Nashville.

Orlando – 1976

--Barbara Roper was on the committee to hire Clark. She was such a stellar volunteer that she went on to become chairman of the national Y board.

--Joe Warwick and his wife, Jean, became our friends when he joined the Central Florida staff. Joe was part of the "turn-around team" who was recruited by Bill Phillips. At that time Florida was just beginning to come out of a deep recession and the Y had been adversely affected. The turn-around was a huge success partly because of Joe.

 --Chief financial officer (CFO), Wayne Brewer, helped to leverage the Ys revenue creating a unique investment program. Wayne went on to join Clark in Chattanooga and they served in Houston together. They remain close friends to this day.

 --Gene Dooley was on the Y staff before being recruited to Ft. Myers. Clark and Gene have been professional and personal friends ever since.

--Cindy Ferguson and Tina Harr were best friends and they spent a lot of good times together with our family. Tina had worked for the church when Clark recruited her to be a part of the Y and went on to be a branch executive and part of the Chattanooga leadership team. Cindy Ferguson is fun, vivacious and dedicated to the Y. She was part of Clark's leadership team in several Ys (she was practically like family), as well as being CEO in Bristol, Tennessee.

She ended her career as VP of programs in Houston.

Chattanooga- 1982

--Spencer Wright, Frank Brock, Jim Robinson, Jim Irvine and John Guerry were part of the board who recruited Clark to come to Chattanooga. They had key board leadership. Clark learned how to work with old money from these stately gentlemen. They opened many opportunities for my husband while he was CEO.

---Lois Ann Frank and Pam Miller were fondly called "Frick and Frack". They worked as a close knit team to take the most mundane and transform it into a thing of beauty. Being in charge of special events and celebrations, they were called upon quite frequently to work their magic.

Nashville--1987

--Clark followed Adrian Moody who was an international Y star and a legend in the movement. He was a wise man who was so sincere and passionate about serving others that when he asked you to help with a task, no one could turn him down.

--Jim Rayhab was the senior member of the staff…he was Clark's Go-to guy. If Clark needed anything, Jim seemed to appear and make it happen. He was a kind and gentle person.

--Central to helping navigate the business and political landscape of the city was Jimmy Webb. He and lawyer, Peter Oldham, were instrumental in acquiring the Maryland Farms Tennis and Racquet Club for the Y.

--Mayor Richard Fulton and his wife, Sandra, both were helpful to Clark during his Nashville tenure. Sandra became board chair and even went on the Russia YMCA International tour with Clark and other Y volunteers.

--Young executives Steve Tarver, Gary Schlansker, and Bob McGaughey were so welcoming when Clark arrived in Nashville. They went on to become CEOs in other cities and remain friends with Clark to this day.

--Clark's last board chair in Nashville was Ron Knox. He

has gone on to become a key player in the association and chaired the YMCA foundation.

--The largest donor in the history of the Nashville Y was entrepreneur Cal Turner. He taught Clark what "joyful giving" is all about.

--The only father/son team Clark ever recruited was George and Scott Goyer. George was Clark's development director and Scott was an executive of the Green Hills Y. George was wise in the area of financial development and Clark gained a great deal of knowledge just being around him.

--Dortch Oldham, Nelson Andrews, Walter Knestrick, Bill Turner, and Cal Turner, Jr. were key board members who helped steer the Nashville Y to become one of largest Ys in the country.

-- Dr. Tom Frist, Jr. was a key philanthropist who was in-strumental in funding early projects at the new Y camp. Dr. Frist used to love to visit camp via his sea plane.

--The head of the Joe C. Davis Foundation, Bill DeLoache, essentially underwrote funding for a new camp which is now the Joe C. Davis Outdoor Center.

--John Ed Miller provided extraordinary leadership and personal friendship, especially during difficult times.

--Our first pastor when we moved to Nashville was Fr. Joe Pat Breen. He became a dear friend and confident. Father was so empathetic and caring to our entire family.

--Clark's Y gang included Larry Stumb, Howard Ander-son, Bill Turner, Bill Bailey, Gail Epley, Ken Klein, Bob Na-pier, Ken Martin, E.B. Smith, and Dick Murphy. This group of Y members and workout buddies became Clark's social outlet. We both have fond memories of gathering with this group and their families.

--Another special group was Clark's Cursillo group. Bill Blaufuss, Bill Gavigan, Steve Mason, Larry DeFrance, Rob Ledger, Joe Williams, Jim Tuerff, and Jack Smithwick were part of a small prayer group who have been meeting weekly together for over 30 years. They are part of Clark's spiritual life.

-- Sr. Mary Angela and The Nashville Dominican Sisters have always been there for Clark. He has been on numerous councils/committees for the sisters.

--Mark Weller and Bob Copeland were two people who helped make the Nashville Y camp a reality.

--Clark thought of Tom and Kim Looby as his dynamic duo. Tom was the true architect of the Joe C Davis Outdoor Center. Kim was the executive the Brentwood Y.

--Clark considers Julie Sistrunk and Lori Swan to be two of his best hires ever. They have stood by him during some of his most challenging times.

--Clark used to call Jay Lawrence his corporate conscience. He was director and founder of Y urban services in Nashville.

--Laurel Wilson, Kathy Ragland, and Jodi Duke-Schroer were what my husband liked to say were Clark's girls. They were his early hires and all are success stories.

--It's obvious that my husband thinks the world of Bill Wilson since this book and Clark's career is dedicated to both him and Bill Phillips. Clark tells me that Bill is one of the most generous and effective board members with whom he has ever worked.

--Florence and Buzz Davis seemed to know everyone, introducing Clark to the "movers and shakers" in the city. The couple personified southern hospitality which caused every one they met eager to give to the Y and other community causes.

Houston- 2002

--Search committee chairman, David Shindeldecker, helped bring Clark to Houston and became his personal friend.

--Mike Logan, another board chair became Clark's confidant, member of the search committee, and personal friend.

--John Duncan was a coach, mentor, philanthropist while Clark was in Houston, and continues to be a dear friend.

--Larry Kellner (former CEO of Continental Airlines) as board chair was one of the most innovative and influential people with whom Clark has ever worked. When Larry was chair, he poised the Y for greatness.

--Devoted to the Y and its mission Scott and Jeni Halliday opened so many doors for the Y. This couple opened their hearts, their home, and their checkbook to the Y. We continue to stay in touch with this vibrant couple.

--As his personal assistant, Mary Norton managed Clark's daily activities. She made sure he got to where he needed to be...she kept his crazy busy schedule and performed countless other tasks. She is one of Clark's trusted friends.

--Mike Hodge was one of the most loyal employees Clark worked with in Houston. His skills in technology were greatly appreciated as well as his friendship.

--Clark considers Jeff Watkins an international genius. His work in this area was outstanding and revealed what the YMCA mission is all about.

--Charles Cleveland and his wife, Sherri- Charles was on Clark's executive team. They were two of our dearest friends while in Houston. The Cleveland's even hosted a bridal shower at their lovely home for our youngest daughter, Caroline.

--Joe and Harriet Foster are so dedicated to the YMCA that they have a facility named after them. Joe was on the search committee and chaired the Y foundation. She and Joe chaired the campaign for the Miracle League which provides adaptive fields for those with special needs. It is now complete and is a fabulous complex largely due to the efforts of this couple.

--"There are angels among us." Clark and I heard this phrase first coined by board chair, Paul VanWagenen, at a YMCA event. We've never forgotten those words as Paul was the board chair who took the Y through some tough financial years. The non-profit fared well partly because of his leadership. He was the "angel among us".

-- Brothers Dick and David Weekley have been incredibly generous to the Y. Clark greatly appreciates their wisdom. One of Houston's most successful Y's is named after the Weekly family.

--Beth Shea was the Houston Y's first female board chair. She became a close friend of Clark's as well as a mentor.

--The Vietnamese Dominican Sisters captured our hearts. Clark worked with them in helping with financial development. We loved being with the Sisters and have been so grateful for all their prayers.

--John Arnoldy is another board member who was a huge support to the Y during Clark's tenure as CEO.

--Former board member, John Poindexter, introduced us to the Big Country in west Texas. Several times we visited his beautifully restored historic Cibolo Creek Ranch. It was a lovely respite from the bustle of the big city of Houston and the stresses that come with being a CEO.

--Rey Gonzales brought much wisdom and Clark valued the cultural diversity to Clark's board. He and Y executive, Marie Arcos, introduced us to the impressive Houston rodeo.

--Clark calls Bob Thomas his main compass while in Houston. He probably gave more money and chaired more committees than any other board member. Clark considers Bob a good friend.

--Byrd Larberg- Clark says, "Byrd is Mr. Mission for the Y and a good friend." He was Clark's final board chair.

Clark feels sure he's left people out whom he should thank. If so, it was totally unintentional as he feels much gratitude for ALL the family, staff, friends, and volunteers with whom he has worked over these past fifty years. May God bless each and every one.